THE SMART HOME

THE NATURAL WAY TO EDUCATE THROUGH PLAY

Shannon Pretorius, M.Ed.

The Smart Home

The author specifically disclaims all responsibility for any liability, loss or risk, personal or otherwise, that is incurred as a consequence, directly or indirectly, of the use and application of the contents of this book.

Copyright ©2010 by Shannon Pretorius

All rights reserved. This book or any portion thereof may not be reproduced or used in any manner whatsoever without the express written permission of the author except for the use of brief quotations in a book review. For information or general questions about any parts of this book, or to contact the author, send an e-mail to the author at: thesmarthomebook@gmail.com

Cover Art Photo:
Foreground: (c)iStockphoto/Alexey Avdeev
Background: Image Copyright Melanie DeFazio, 2011
           Used under license from Shutterstock.com

Cover Font: (c)dafont/Billy Argel

ISBN 978-0-615-47345-1

Shannon Pretorius

TABLE OF CONTENTS

DEDICATION	4
INTRODUCTION	5
CHAPTER 1 - BATHTUB SCIENCE	7
CHAPTER 2 - THE CHALLENGE OF CHORES	18
CHAPTER 3 - OUTDOOR ADVENTURE	26
CHAPTER 4 - KEEP YOUR EYES ON THE ROAD	37
CHAPTER 5 - HIDDEN PICTURES	56
CHAPTER 6 - READ BETWEEN THE LINES	66
CHAPTER 7 - YEAH WRITE, MOM!	78
CHAPTER 8 - SO MUCH TO DO, SO LITTLE TIME!	88
CHAPTER 9 - PLAYING WITH YOUR FOOD	98
SAFE COOKING - KIDS IN THE KITCHEN	111
101 **NO COST** ACTIVITIES FOR FAMILIES	118
WORDS TO THE WISE	131

DEDICATION

This book is dedicated to the millions of parents out there who want so badly to give their kids the very best but feel like they lack time, money, resources, or know-how.

I want to thank my husband, Theo, for encouraging me to write this book, for not judging my authorship abilities, and for doing all of the research on the business side. I am especially thankful to my daughter, Mia, who is alive with wonder about life and people and the world in which she lives. Thank you to my siblings and my parents for their interest in my literary journey, and particularly to my mom for taking the time to edit my drafts. To my social media friends who responded to status updates regarding book-related inquiries, and to friends and family who took the time to read through my very rough draft and give me feedback; this product wouldn't be the same without you. Lastly, thank YOU for reading my thoughts, tips, and suggestions, and for welcoming them into your home. Enjoy the reading, but more importantly, enjoy the wonders of learning with your child.

Shannon

Shannon Pretorius

INTRODUCTION

This is a book about the everyday routines and rituals that your family engages in and how you can inject educational vocabulary, activities, mindset, and play into those routines naturally, with little or no cost. That's the way to edu-play.

Today's generation of kids are being taught differently than their parents were taught. There has been more brain research, we know more about different learning styles and intelligences, and there is more value placed on real world application of skills. What better place to include education then in each child's individual, real world-the life they are living. Families don't have a lot of down time in their days. Kids are engrossed in their school day, extracurricular activities, social lives, and homework. Parents are juggling jobs, family life, chauffeuring of kids from one place to another, and are still searching for more hours when the day is done.

I wrote this book because I am a working mother and a teacher and I understand the precious value of your time with your family. As a mother, I want to make sure that I give my child the experiences that will help her grow, learn, and thrive in life, school, and every journey in which she partakes. As a teacher, I want my child to feel comfortable and enjoy the learning process that will be an ongoing part of her life. I feel that the more I can do with her naturally at home, the more she will embrace the idea of lifelong learning and the easier it will be for her.

The Smart Home

As a natural educator, I was attracted to the field of education because I believe strongly in educating parents alongside children. No child can traverse this world alone, and no parent can teach their child everything without a little help from the world around them. I am reaching out to all parents who think there must be a better way, a quicker way, a cheaper way, a more interesting way, or an easier way to be a part of educating and building experiences with their kids in the comfort of their already full lives.

Inspiration for this book came when I started itching to have a broader impact on education, while not being able to put my finger on a job that would give me that type of satisfaction. As I finished writing down my thoughts as to how parents, including myself, could incorporate teaching within their everyday interactions with their children, I realized that sharing these ideas and suggestions, in the form of a book, had the potential of having exactly the type of impact I was hoping to make. Reaching beyond the classroom and straight into the home can make all the difference, for in the home is where the impacts of life lessons are taken to heart.

I hope you enjoy this book, and more than that, I hope the few ideas presented here will open the flood gates to the many opportunities available to you and your children that you stumble over everyday.

Chapter One

Bathtub Science

Children need to bathe or shower at some point during the week whether they like it or not. Whether that time is meant to be a Monday morning wake-up call, a Wednesday after school relaxation time, or a Friday night degreaser, science fits naturally here. Once you start rounding up some ordinary household items for these bathtub science experiments, kids' minds will become quite inventive and will take off. Be ready to watch their creativity soar!

Popular Vocabulary that Might Come to the Surface

absorb, float, sink, predict, measure, volume, submerge, mixture, settle, solution, solvent, syringe, dissolve, flow, soak, surface tension, water, water cycle, acid, base, depth, control, experiment

WARNING: KIDS NEED SUPERVISION IN THE BATH TUB. IT IS YOUR JOB TO MONITOR WHAT GOES IN AND COMES OUT. ELECTRICAL ITEMS MAY BE ENTICING TO KIDS BUT THEY DO NOT BELONG ANYWHERE NEAR WATER. IN ADDITION, SMALL ITEMS THAT CAN GO DOWN THE DRAIN CAN CLOG THE PLUMBING SYSTEM. PLEASE TAKE PRECAUTION AND MONITOR YOUR CHILDREN IN THE TUB. ALWAYS ERR ON THE SIDE OF CAUTION!!! SAFETY FIRST!!

The Smart Home

THERE IS A SEA OF OPPORTUNITIES, BUT HERE ARE A FEW SUGGESTIONS

1. Encourage kids to collect a container to hold water and some absorbable objects from around the house such as different size sponges, a paper towel, a napkin, a tissue, a kitchen towel or a washcloth, a sock, and any other objects you have that will soak up water. Their goal will be to see how much water these objects can absorb by letting them soak in as much water as possible and then squeezing the object out completely into the desired container. They can test to see how many times they have to squeeze the object to fill the container, or they can measure which object fills the container the highest when squeezed just once. Guide them to think about how size, thickness, and material might have made a difference in the amount of water absorbed during this experiment. They can also time how long it takes for each object to soak in the water. To change the activity, kids can try objects that don't seem to have as much absorbency (cloth napkins, a pillow case, a piece of paper...).

2. Allow your child to take a few of his favorite (water-friendly) toys into the tub for a little test of float and sink. Before beginning, he/she can separate the toys into two piles based on a hypothesis of which ones will float and which ones will sink. Then he can line them up according to how quickly each one in the "sink" pile will take to get to the bottom of the tub. Note whether the toys were organized by weight, density, or by size. Then, bombs away! They can test each one and see what happens and then see if the results differ if the toys are dropped from higher up. (You might get a nice splash going this time, so make sure the curtain or shower door is closed first!) Will the floating objects plunge below the surface first and then rise to the top again, or will the surface tension of the water stop them or slow them down? Which objects

will stay submerged? For a different spin on things, suggest that they float one of the small toys on the surface of the water and make circles in the water with a finger around the toy to create currents. Their purpose is to try to get the toy to drift to one end of the tub without touching it. They can compare the size, weight, and density of the objects and decide which factors had the greatest effects on their results. Kids can also note which object sinks fastest, and ask of the objects that float, do they remain floating the entire time, or do some of them become water-logged and sink after some time? Lastly, they can consider what would have to change with an object to cause it to have the opposite result.

3. Get out the turkey baster, medicine syringe, (no needles, of course) and some plastic measuring cups or spoons for some testing fun. Allow kids to see how many syringes it takes to fill one of the measuring cups or test the surface tension of the water by using the baster to fill one of the measuring spoons. How many drops does it take before the surface tension breaks and the water flows over the edge? Measuring in this activity is the key! Kids can try these activities by filling bigger containers using a syringe, teaspoon, tablespoon, or baster. How many of each does it take? Determine which container has the best rim for "overfilling" and let them make a hypothesis as to why it is the best. Then they can decide which tool they would use to gather chocolate syrup (or another favorite sweet) if they were given only 30 seconds. Why that one?

4. Bubbles and bubbles and bubbles, oh my! Help your child collect as many kinds of soap as you can from around the house. Bar soap, hand soap, foamy soap, dish soap, laundry soap, bubble bath, etc. Then give them some Tupperware® or plastic bowls of some kind in the bath, too. They can have fun mixing different

kinds of soap in the containers to see which one makes the most bubbles. Use a medicine dropper or a measuring cup to measure the amount of both soap and water they add to each container. They should make predictions first, of course! Then the kids can compare the cloudiness of the soapy solution in each container as well and determine which one bubbles or foams the fastest and which one needs to be shaken or mixed the longest before it foams. Lastly, kids can skim the bubbles off the top of the water and see which pile of bubbles disintegrates the fastest and which one holds on the longest in their hands.

5. Baths are meant to get us clean, but this activity might leave your little one dirtier than when he/she started. Gather some items to mix with water such as a handful of dirt, a tablespoon of sugar, some flour or corn starch, maybe some bread crumbs or a piece of stale bread, or whatever else is in the house that you are willing to let them put into the tub. Have the kids try mixing one item at a time into a container of water, stirring it up and observing what happens. Does it dissolve into the water as a solvent? What happens when they stop stirring? Does the mixture separate and settle to the bottom of the container? Note similarities between trials that dissolve in the water and trials that mix and then separate again when they stop stirring. Encourage them to survey others before conducting their experiment to get their hypothesis of the results they will find. Consider what would happen if hot water versus cold water was used in the experiment. This activity could also be completed outside or in a sink.

If your child would like to try using hot water, please make sure they have help from an adult to conduct the experiment. Hot water can burn skin and cause injury. Don't experiment with your health!

6. Playing with your food may not always be allowed at the dinner table, but it can be allowed in the tub. Allow your child to bring some leftover food scraps from dinner into the bath. Then put some water in different containers and place one piece of food in each. See what has happened to each piece of food by the end of the bath. Did the food pieces dissolve? Did they float or sink in the water? What changes did the food go through? Did the temperature of the water make a difference? Did the size of the food morsel make a difference? What happens when they stir or mix up the food? How could they change the experiment next time? Determine which food groups dissolve best in the water. Encourage kids to consider what is happening to that same food in their stomach after they eat it. Of course kids can also survey others to see what factors they felt caused different reactions in the experiment.

Just six ideas regarding what can be done to encourage the use of science in the bathtub were listed here. There are millions of other trials and experiments that can be conducted while getting clean in the tub or shower. Here are some suggestions of things that might be found around the house that could be fun to put in the bathtub. You and your child can use your imaginations to help determine what to do with them!

The Smart Home

HOUSEHOLD ITEMS TO EXPLORE IN THE TUB!

- Plastic measuring cups and spoons
- Paper products
- Legos® (make sure they are not small enough to go down the drain)
- A brush or comb
- Foam shapes and letters
- Sponges or a small cloth
- Plastic baggies
- Beach toys
- A watering can
- A strainer
- Marbles (careful-they could go down the drain)
- Play dough
- Fabric scraps
- Buttons
- Tweezers
- A turkey baster

- A ladle
- Cotton balls
- Empty plastic food containers
- Hard, plastic toys
- Food coloring mixed with water
- Cookie cutters
- Ice cubes or ice cube trays
- Old toothbrushes
- Empty spray bottles
- Goggles
- Balls-bouncy balls, golf balls, basketballs, Nerf® balls, etc.
- Dry foods or dry baking products
- Aluminum foil

The Smart Home

THE PARENTS' ROLE IN BATH TIME

Your job while the kids are having fun splashing around with household objects is to foster the experiments and the process by engaging in questioning and hypothesizing with your child and using the vocabulary you want them to learn. Question which objects will hold the most water and which ones will withstand the fill-and-squeeze process. Make guesses prior to the experiments as to how they will each turn out in the end. Teach your kids how to conduct experiments and how to use controls in experiments where applicable. Encourage them to create their own questions and then figure out answers to them through their exploration and experimentation.

In addition to engaging in the wonders of the fun, as the parent, it is your job to give your child the time to host the trials. Bath time can be a great way to unwind and relax before bedtime. If you are short on time, try offering dessert in the bath (popsicles, pudding or ice cream on a stick work great for that), or read to your child in the bathtub instead of in bed after the bath. If that doesn't work, try doubling up on bath time with younger or same-sex siblings to avoid the line at the bathroom door. Still struggling to find time for bath time fun? Decide which days you will allow different experiments. If Saturday is wide open, allow more Bathtub Science time on that day! Don't be afraid of mid-day baths either. Who says bath time always has to take place in the morning or as the last event of the day? Does your child have a low homework load on Thursdays? That's a perfect day for homework time in the bathtub with some science fun!

Are you cooking dinner, checking e-mail, paying bills, or doing another task while your child is in the tub? No problem. Use five minutes immediately following bath time to talk with your child about what happened in the tub. Show your enthusiasm by the tone of your voice when you ask specific, open-ended questions (those that can't be answered with a yes/no response), by using eye contact when they explain what happened, and by wondering aloud how they might change the experiment next time. Can't find the time right after the bath? How about getting a journal for your child to jot down their excitement and results of what happened. Younger kids can draw pictures of their experiments and the outcomes and add captions later. When you finally settle down for the night, read the observations and respond, in writing, with your thoughts and excitement about the trials. Not only will your child be excited to see what you write back to them, but you will have just opened up a great line of communication with your child and you will encourage journaling and the power of writing in the meantime! Is that too old-fashioned for you? Try e-mailing or texting each other instead. Still not working for you? If you have older kids, how about starting a family blog where others can respond about the science fun as well as engage in discussions regarding other topics.

Bath time isn't the only time that this vocabulary can be used. As the other chapters in this book will show, the same vocabulary can be incorporated into many other situations and adventures that you and your family embark on in your everyday lives!

The Smart Home

CHAPTER GLOSSARY

absorb - soak up

acid - something that has a ph value of 7 or less; something sour

base - a compound that reacts with an acid

control - the part of two experiments that remains the same for testing purposes

currents - a flow of something, like water

depth - how deep something is

disintegrate - to break apart or deteriorate

dissolve - to become absorbed in a liquid solution

drift - to move naturally with a current

experiment - a test or trial to try to find something out

float - stay on the surface of the water

flow - to move in one direction or to circulate

hypothesis - an educated guess

measure - to see what amount you have

mixture - a combination or blend of different things

observe - to watch

predict - make a projection or guess

Shannon Pretorius

settle - to sink gradually

sink - go to the bottom of the container

soak - to be completely wet

solution - the molecular mixture of any two things

solvent - a substance that dissolves in another substance

submerge - sink below the surface of the water

surface tension - the elastic-like force on the surface of a liquid

syringe - a tube that has a suction component that can bring liquid in and push it out

temperature - how hot or cold something is

volume - the amount of space an object takes up

water cycle - the natural sequence of water passing through the atmosphere, coming to the ground as a liquid, and then evaporating into the atmosphere again

Chapter Two

The Challenge of Chores

The dreaded weekend essential; the word that's sure to get a groan: chores! This chapter is to help make chores a little less daunting and slightly more interesting for kids (and maybe even for you). Because kids of different ages might not be completing the same chores as each other, these ideas won't fit everyone, but you will get the picture and I am confident that you will be able to take what I give you and run with it!

Is the Word Chore in Your Vocabulary?

Yes, there is even vocabulary associated with chores. Here, a list of chores is accompanied by educational words that match the job.

- Dishes - temperature, organization, absorb, submerge, matter, settle, separate, mixture, cycle, float, sink, dissolve, chemical/physical change, soak, shape, size, sort, durability, dilute, melt, opposites (clean/dirty, wet/dry, small/large)

- Trash - combine, odor, weight, decompose, recycle, reuse, gather, strength, durability, condense, compare, sour, base, acid, solid, liquid, gas

- Laundry - symmetrical, flat, texture, sort, temperature, size, color, liquid, solid, gas, separate, organization, lint, soil, soak, dissolve, property, wet, damp, dry, steam, water vapor, sound, pitch, speed, rotate

Shannon Pretorius

- Dusting - cling, clockwise, counter clockwise, under/over, static, kinetic energy, momentum, motion, friction, force, gravity, arm span, area, shape, dust

- Making the Bed - shape, even, layers, top/bottom, symmetry, equivalent, textures, midpoint, buoyant, capacity

- Bathroom - rotate, clockwise, counter clockwise, volume, angles, speed, organisms, sections, parts/whole, force, flow, water cycle, depth, source, odor, scent, plug/plunge, gravity

- Vacuuming - suction, force, energy, motion, pattern, function, lever, gear, conductor, source, receiver, tension, vibration, capacity, range, rotate, work

- Pick Up Toys/Room - gravity, organization, sort, capacity, shape, size, area, angles, minimum, maximum, mass

- Feed Pets - amount, time, measurements-cup, half cup, nutrients, greater than/less than, solid, liquid, equal, mixture, texture, variety

- Water Plants - roots, leaves, stem, flower, liquid, measure, amount, soak, dirt, soil, absorb, nutrients, photosynthesis, fertilize

- Clear or Set the Table - full/empty, balance, compare/contrast, order, shape, diameter, area, object, purpose, even/odd, degrees, left/right, above/below, colors

The Smart Home

A Fresh Look at Chores

1. Do chores ABC style. Start at the beginning of the alphabet and work through the alphabetical list of chores until you get to the end. Some chores will be in the list more than once under a different letter. Knowing they are headed somewhere and giving an order to the chores will introduce kids to new tasks and allow exploration of words, too! Of course all 26 chores will not be completed in one day. Just check them off as chore times come and go!

The following ABC Chore List may not work for you; it is only a guide. Replace any listed chores with other chores that fit your household as needed, or simply use this as a reference and as a family, make your own ABCs!

A - aroma: find the smelliest place in the house and clean it!

B - bathroom duty: clean the tub, sink, counter, and toilet

C - clean your room

D - dust all wood in the house

E - eat: feed the pets in the house

F - food: help with dinner preparations and clean up

G - glass: wash all mirrors and glass inside the house

H - high: clean things up high-fan blades or tops of blinds or window coverings

I - interior decorations: wipe down décor on shelves

J - jungle: water plants in the house and outside

K - kitchen: clean the counters, sink, and microwave

L - laundry: sort it and put it away

M - mop the living room and dining room

N - "no" pile: make a pile of toys/clothes to give away that you have grown out of

O - organize your bedroom and toys

P - pick up toys and things out of place

Q - quilt: make your bed

R - rugs: shake them out and vacuum them

S - set the table

T - trash duty!

U - unload the dishwasher or clothes dryer

V - vacuum any room you want

W - wash four windows

X - x-ray eyes see germs: wipe light switches, door knobs, keyboards, phones

Y - yard: pull weeds, cut the grass, or trim the bushes

Z - zoo: dust stuffed animals by taking them outside and shaking them off

The Smart Home

2. You pick for me and I pick for you. Let the kids pick which chores you will do for the day and you pick theirs! You may do this from a list of approved choices, or just roll with it. Let the kids pick for each other, too. They can each make a list of 2-3 chores and then YOU get to assign who completes which list. Lessons about fairness and trust will naturally arise here.

3. This next idea is great if you are in a hurry and just need the place whipped into shape fast. Play musical chores. Assign everyone a chore. Blast some music. When the music stops, everyone stops their chore and runs to someone else's chore. Start the music again and start the chore where the last person left off. In 10 minutes, everyone will have helped to complete many chores and a speed cleaning will be achieved. WARNING: I WOULD **NOT** ADVISE INCLUDING CHORES THAT REQUIRE GENTLE HANDS ON FRAGILE ITEMS WITH THIS GAME. IT'S JUST TOO EXCITING, AND SOMETHING IS BOUND TO BREAK!

4. The un-chore. Need the sliding doors or windows washed? Make it a game. Play mime with you on one side of the door and a child on the other side. Each armed with your own cloth and cleaner, their job is to copy your moves as you clean. Both sides of the glass will get cleaned at the same time. Need the wood or tile floors touched up? Put on some old socks and spray cleaner on the bottom of them. Everyone will have fun skating around the floor, slipping and sliding while the floor gets clean. To pick up toys, have a scavenger hunt. Each person has to find something blue, something round, something wooden, or something that makes noise. When they return with each item, you direct them to the appropriate place to put it. Chores will be finished in no time and more fun will be had then you ever thought possible.

5. Chores are always more fun when they are completed together. Make yourselves into an amoeba, attached together at all times, and go from room to room sharing the clean-up job. Laugh at the challenges of maneuvering as one, problem-solve how to get everything done in one room as a group and practice patience and balance as you help one another.

6. Chores are tiring. Make energy meters (like thermometers that measure energy) for each person in the house. You can use regular paper and markers for this. When you see someone working really hard, their energy will be fading, so fade it on their energy meter. When their energy gets too low, they can come refuel with a special snack or treat before continuing their chore. After everyone is finished with their chores, all the energy meters will be quite low. Restore that energy by watching a family show together, treating yourselves to a special snack, or having some family time with books.

Whatever the chore, there is bound to be something that you can do to spice it up and make it new again. Be safe, have fun and most of all, remember that kids are kids and their standard of clean is not the same as yours. Thank them for their help, admire what they have done, notice how hard they tried and how proud they are, and don't criticize a well-intended effort. We all struggle to try again when we "fail" the first time. Children (as well as adults) tend to enjoy what they do and to improve how they do it when their efforts are met with positive recognition. Criticizing their work will surely lead to unwilling little workers. Showing appreciation of their efforts and accomplishments, on the other hand, will help build self-esteem, pride in a job well done, and a solid work ethic.

The Smart Home

PARENTS PLAY A BIG ROLE IN CHORES

We all have a standard for how we expect chores to be completed at home and yet most of us hate completing them to that standard ourselves. The laundry is never done, there are always dishes that need to be put away, and the bathrooms seem to have a life of their own. You are tripping over toys and slipping on clothes and sitting on who knows what. You need help! Kids should be helping with chores. It is up to you to decide what is appropriate for each one of your kids to handle. Instilling the ideas of responsibility to the household, respect for space, safety of cleanliness, and feeling of accomplishment are all valuable lessons that kids learn from doing chores. Whether your two-year-old is helping to pick up toys or your four-year-old is making her bed and clearing the table, or your ten-year-old is vacuuming the carpets and cleaning the bathrooms, there are chores to suit every person at every age.

There are some chores that we always dread. Make a list of basic chores that need to be completed weekly. Then make a broader list of "extra" chores or seasonal chores. Work with your kids to find out which chores they prefer to complete (my daughter LOVES to dust-go figure). Then find some tools that are age appropriate for them to use to complete the chore. For younger kids, a feather duster or micro fiber pad works well for dusting while disinfecting wipes are great for quick bathroom cleaning or wiping down door knobs and light switches. A cloth sweeper is wonderful for wood or tile floors with a wet pad for quick mopping. Glass wipes can easily be used on glass top surfaces or windows. As kids get older or if you have more natural, gentle cleaners, they can use spray cleaners and paper towels. If the kids can shop with you for the necessary supplies, or be on the alert for when it's time to get refills, or help pick out the type of cleaners they want to use, they will take more ownership of the task and enjoy it more.

Your biggest job here will be to make sure you provide some variety and choice to everyone involved. Does everyone have to make their own bed? Can one person do all the beds because it's their favorite job? Sometimes kids are most comfortable doing the same job every night or every week. Other times they are so bored with the chore that they can't wait to try something new. New is exciting! New is fun! New is only new once or twice. Change it up when you can to keep it new!

Enjoy your new outlook on chores. I hope chore day is coming soon while the energy and excitement are still there!

Chapter 3

Outdoor Adventure

Sometimes the great outdoors can be more overwhelming then pleasing when you are looking for something to do, but when approached from a new angle, hopefully you will find fun and adventure and maybe even learn something new about your own outdoor space when you try some new outdoor adventures. Don't feel confined to your own property though. There is a whole world of wonder out there ready to be explored whether it's in the dead of winter or during the peak of summer. Just don't trespass onto private property!

Popular Related Vocabulary to Bury Yourself In

temperature, Fahrenheit, Celsius, living/non-living, texture, motion, ramp, flower, root, stem, leaf, nutrient, soil, solar, cirrus, cumulus, stratus clouds, weather, silt, life cycle, metamorphosis, wind, habitat, organism, momentum, erosion, weathering, rocks, minerals, environment, landform, sediments, river, sea level, flood, flood plain, channel, meander, map, key, scale

WARNING: THE GREAT OUTDOORS REALLY ARE GREAT, BUT CAN BE DANGEROUS, TOO. KIDS NEED SUPERVISION WHEN LEAVING YOUR PROPERTY AND SOMETIMES EVEN WHEN STAYING ON YOUR PROPERTY. PLEASE DISCUSS ALL EXPERIMENTS, AREAS, AND DANGER WITH YOUR CHILDREN AND DON'T BE AFRAID TO SET LIMITS! IF YOU DON'T KNOW WHAT YOU ARE GETTING INTO, RESEARCH IT FIRST OR TAKE A PRO WITH YOU.

Shannon Pretorius

GETTING TO KNOW MOTHER NATURE

1. For younger kids, the written parts of this activity can be completed in picture form or verbally.

When it's time to play outside, give your child a piece of paper and a pencil and guide him to stand in one spot and look around. The idea here is to encourage the kids to write down what they see and speculate (guess) why those things are there. They can look up, down, and all around. Once a good list is written, it's time to move in for a closer look. Start with the items on the list that can be touched. See if your son/daughter can make further observations about what is seen. Can he/she list six details about each item using their senses? (Make sure he knows not to taste anything.) Once that is done, tackle the items that can't be touched. What details can be written down about those items? Challenge the kids to write down four details for each written entry. When that list is complete, encourage a new list to be made detailing three things anyone can do to help preserve the natural environment around us. Encourage sharing of these discoveries with the family.

2. Help your child make a line graph to chart temperature variation. Start with a large L on a piece of paper. Along the bottom, write the days of the week. Label the left side, using equidistant numbers to represent temperature. Each day, look at an outdoor thermometer (at the same time of day if possible) and chart the temperature reading with a dot. At the end of the week, connect the dots. You and your child can compare graphs from week to week to note seasonal changes, or if you want to have the graph continue through the month, extend the bottom line and write numbers for each day of the month along the bottom.

The Smart Home

3. Cloud watching is a fun, easy, relaxing activity for the whole family. Get a blanket, find a good spot in the yard, at the park, etc., lay back and look up. See who can find cirrus, cumulus, and stratus clouds. What shapes are in the clouds? What objects can be found? Make determinations such as which direction the clouds are moving- north, south, east, or west. For younger kids, are they moving up, down, toward my feet, or past my head? How strong is the wind that is moving them? Talk about the different shades of color of the clouds and why some are puffy while some appear to be streaks.

4. Outside, living things are all around us. Give your little one a glass jar to collect some small living things (don't forget about plants). Use plastic wrap or foil for the top of the jar and poke some small holes into the top for air. Help him identify the insects, plants, and creepy crawlies that he collected. Encourage him to draw a picture of each one. For bugs, count how many body parts they have. Together, locate different features such as wings, eyes, stingers (be careful!), and count the number of legs. For plants, flowers, and grasses, look carefully (sometimes the bottom of a glass jar can act as a magnifying glass) to find the veins, pedals, stem, etc. See if your child can pull up a weed with the roots still attached. Talk about the job of each of the 4 main parts of a plant (root, stem, leaf, and flower). What parts of the plant have soil on them? Why? Are there any insect eggs on the leaves you collected? Look up the life cycle of the animals collected. Be sure you sets the bugs free when you are done!

5. Get down and dirty! Dirt is everywhere and usually even ends up in places where we don't want it! Let the kids collect some dirt in a plastic cup. If they see more than one kind of dirt (dirt of different color, texture, or particle size) they can collect a sample of

each kind. Let each child feel the dirt, shake the dirt, and look closely at what is in it. How does each dirt sample differ from the next? Using a watering can, add some water to each sample and observe what happens. Does the water soak in or just lay on top? Now allow the kids to gather some uncooked dried bean seeds (or some other raw seed from a plant you ate for dinner last night) and plant one seed in each dirt cup. Place it on the porch or somewhere where it will get some sunlight and wait. Give your kids the responsibility of watering it daily. See if anything grows. Pose these questions to your little scientist: Why did one seed grow better than the others? Why did it grow in that kind of dirt?

6. Find an area that you all like to visit (a park, nature trail, playground, etc.). Give your child the materials needed to make a map of the area that includes a compass rose, key, and a scale. If there is water near the area, label the body of water. Then examine the area around the water with your child. Has it been affected by weathering or erosion? What organisms (any living things) can be found in this special place? Once the map is complete, take note of when you were there. Come back on a different day or at a different time and take note of whether the sounds you are hearing are the same or different. This is a great way to encourage observation of the area around you, finding subtle differences in nature, and finding out what's really living in your region.

The six activities in this chapter are examples of ways to edu-play outdoors. Of course there are many other ways that you can appreciate and learn from Mother Nature. On the next page you will find some suggestions of when and how to encourage outdoor adventure. Let these topics be guides for you to mesh into your life, comfort level, and area that you live.

The Smart Home

FAMILY SUGGESTIONS FOR SAMPLING OUTDOOR FUN

- Measure the length of the grass, flowers, plants, etc. around you. See how fast they grow and how much they change in a week or a month's time.

- During rainy season (or snowy season), put a bucket outside with some kind of measuring device in it. Measure the amount of rain/snow that you collect in the container and document that in a daily journal. Now what can you use that water/snow for?

- Have fun in the sprinkler while you water the plants and lawn.

- Build a bird house and take pictures of the birds that come to feed there. Look up the species and label your pictures. See how the types of birds change as the seasons change. Create your own bird book with your pictures.

- Take a nature walk and collect interesting items from nature along the way. Press fallen leaves and flowers in wax paper to preserve them. Use that as a bookmark. Arrange pinecones, shiny rocks, and other larger finds in a bowl as a table or mantle centerpiece.

- Lie on the grass and watch the world go by as you use your senses to take in your surroundings.

- Put a dab of honey or sugar water in a plastic container and place it on an outside table, deck, or patio. See what kinds of critters are attracted to it.

- Make a bird feeder with a pinecone, peanut butter, and bird seed.

- Make a hopscotch board on the sidewalk or driveway. Make up different ways to play the game.

- Make a sundial using everyday objects you find in the house.

- Go outside in the rain and splash in the puddles just for fun! Avoid this if there is thunder and lightning.

- Sketch out and plant a floral or vegetable garden.

- Wrap yourself in a blanket and listen to your bedtime story outside while gazing at the stars.

- Follow a star map to locate star constellations or make up your own with groups of stars you see as you sit outside one night. (These are great winter activities since it is darker earlier in the winter.)

- Dig in the yard to see what kinds of soil layers and what kinds of creatures live below your feet. Draw pictures of what you find.

- Roll down a hill. Time yourself and measure your distance over time.

- Walk around the neighborhood looking for signs of weathering and erosion. Take pictures or take notes about what is seen and check back again in a week or a month. What changed during that time? What do you predict will

The Smart Home

be different the next time that spot is visited?

- Explore some different landforms in your area. See how many different landforms you can find as you ride your bike or take a walk.

- Spend the afternoon pretending to be a small animal to get a different perspective about life. What challenges would you face and how could you overcome them?

- Take samples or pictures of the plants and trees in your yard and then look them up to see just what you are living with!

- Learn more about weather by graphing morning, noon, and night temperature readings, cloud coverage, and wind speed. How do these change as the seasons change?

- Make a map of the area you live including street names. Plot a route and ride it. Then revise your map with landmarks you saw along the way. Expand your map with each new bike ride you take.

- Climb a tree. What do you see now?

- Build a fort/animal home from fallen leaves, twigs, etc.

- Plant a tree.

THE PARENTS' ROLE IN OUTDOOR FUN

Your role while the kids are having fun exploring the outdoors and getting dirty is again to engage in explanations of what you see them learning as well as questioning and hypothesizing to encourage your kids to continue exploring. Question what will happen if they leave a certain toy outside over time and it is exposed to the weather elements. Make hypotheses prior to starting an exploration as to what they will find and what they will learn from the experience. Talk about outdoor safety and dangers outdoors such as poison ivy, poisonous berries, sun safety, and stranger danger! You will soon find yourself enjoying more outdoor time as well and will also enjoy more quiet time inside while the kids are out!

Additionally, engaging in exploration and wonder with your child, and taking family trips to places that will encourage that exploration, are essential. The more exposure to new things and to different places that they are given, the more curious and excited they will become about new discoveries. Not everyone is naturally outdoorsy, but as a family, you can create your own adventures that fit your family's lifestyle. Meal time is the perfect time to connect with your family and interact without interruption, so how about eating outside? Time and weather are always concerns, but the more *natural* opportunities your family finds to spend outdoors, instilling vocabulary and helping with planning and organization of events, the more you will find yourself appreciating these opportunities. Watch weather reports and plan accordingly. Double up on activities by doing homework outside, reading stories together outside, having the kids explore while you are gardening or mowing the lawn, or take the laptop outside to get your work done so you can enjoy the outdoors yourself! Don't limit yourself just to your yard. Get everyone moving by combining exercise time with science as you walk or bike together during a nature walk. Whatever you decide to do to encourage this outdoor edu-play, make sure you play an active part in it and are honestly interested in the discussions, conclusions, and interactions your family is encountering in nature.

Are allergies or other issues keeping you inside? Bring the outdoor adventures in. Help prepare maps, charts, graphs, make birdhouses, assemble parts, and test theories inside. You can still be part of the fun without stepping out of your comfort zone. Be open to your kids bringing the outdoors in to show you what they have discovered and learned. Create a space indoors where they are allowed to bring their outdoor treasures. It may be a garage, porch, mud room, laundry room, patio, etc.

Remember to infuse the vocabulary of outdoor fun into other times as well. Driving is a great time to notice the outdoors and interact with the language. Go to the library and find some books about nature. Look for books specific to the area that you live. Learn new things together and remember that it's okay not to know an answer. Look it up together. Kids love stumping their parents. (A little outdoor pun there.) The more you try different things, the more naturally they will fit into what you do everyday. However you decide to incorporate these ideas into your family's lifestyle and routines is up to you. Just remember to keep trying. What a great way to entice your kids to explore and enjoy some time outside instead of in front of the TV or a video game!

Shannon Pretorius

CHAPTER GLOSSARY

Celsius - a temperature scale in which 0 degrees is freezing

channel - the bed of a stream, river, or other waterway

cirrus - a high altitude, thin, white cloud

cumulus - a dense, puffy cloud

environment - the world around you

erosion - the process of things being worn away as a result of natural elements

Fahrenheit - a temperature scale in which 32 degrees is freezing

graph - a diagram showing a connection between things

habitat - the natural environment of an organism; where something lives

key - a table that explains symbols on a map

landform - a feature on the surface of the earth, such as plains, plateaus, mountains, hills, etc.

life cycle - the continuous changes that an organism goes through

living - something that grows and needs nutrition

meander - to take a winding or indirect course

metamorphosis - a change in form or structure

momentum - force or speed of movement

The Smart Home

motion - movement

non-living - an object that does not need nutrition and does not grow

nutrient - something that provides nourishment

organism - a form of life

ramp - an inclined sloping surface

scale - comparing measurements on a map to actual distances

silt - earthy matter like fine sand

stratus - a large, dark, low cloud

texture - the way a surface feels or looks

thorax - the part of the body between the head and abdomen

veins - one of the strands or bundles of tissue that form a leaf

weather - the changing patterns of temperature, wind, and cloud coverage

weathering - decomposing of material due to chemical or mechanical reasons

wind - the movement of air

CHAPTER 4

KEEP YOUR EYES ON THE ROAD

Many of us spend hours and hours each week in the car commuting to work, carting the kids to and from all their activities and friends' houses, or traveling around town to get our errands completed. If you are going to be stuck in a confined area, and you are with your kids, you might as well turn that time into edu-play time. No one has anywhere else to be at that moment, and we all know that time flies when you're having fun!

This chapter is set up differently. Since there are many stationary activities that can be done in the car to improve skills in many different areas, this chapter is set up to focus on different subject areas and how you can play with each one while traveling.

WARNING (YOU KNEW THAT WAS COMING): DRIVING IS AN ACTIVITY THAT REQUIRES YOUR ATTENTION AND TIME. DO NOT COMPROMISE YOUR SAFETY OR THE SAFETY OF OTHERS WHILE COMPLETING THESE ACTIVITIES. ALWAYS PAY ATTENTION TO THE ROAD!

The Smart Home

LITERARY ACTIVITIES

1. Audio books are a great way to enjoy literature together and allow you the flexibility to pause the story for discussions as well. (Audio books also keep the arguing down regarding what music to listen to!) Take turns choosing audio books from the library. Describe to each other how you picture the characters and the setting. When you stop somewhere and turn off the car, summarize what you heard and make predictions about what will happen next. Make connections to the characters or the adventure by sharing something similar that happened to you or to someone you know.

2. Play an alphabet game by having kids find words on signs that start with each letter of the alphabet. See how far you can get in a day.

3. Make sayings or phrases out of the letters on license plates. For example, if the plate starts with PPQ, the phrase could be People Pass Quickly or Please Play Quietly. Make wacky phrases, too!

4. Categorize businesses that you pass. Name a topic and see how many businesses you can find that would fit under that heading.

5. Play a rhyming game to see how many words you can come up with that rhyme with a starter word. For younger kids, word families are good to use here.

6. Pick a category and go around the car naming items that belong in that category until no one can think of any more. Examples of categories would be fruits, states, ice cream flavors, etc.

7. Have the kids read to you! Unless they get car sick, reading in the car is a wonderful way to pass the time. You can certainly talk about the book and discuss the author's purpose or point of view while listening.

8. Practice fluency with tongue twisters. See how many times you can repeat the same alliteration without fumbling your words.

9. Read road signs and billboards aloud to practice word identification.

10. Listen to music and point out rhyming lyrics. Talk about the feelings that might have inspired the artist to write the song. Make up your own verse to the music.

11. Tell a progressive story. One person starts with an introduction sentence. Each person then adds a new part to the story. Keep going around until the story is complete.

12. Develop a "hand story" that goes along with what you are seeing outside as you drive. Start with a topic sentence (the thumb), then add three details (next three fingers) and end with a closing sentence (the pinky).

13. Describe objects you see out the window using as many descriptive words as you can. Someone else can guess what you are describing.

The Smart Home

14. Use travel time for kids to write in their personal journals.

15. Make up acrostic poems creating a word or phrase with each letter in the name of restaurants, businesses, or objects that you pass. Make up Haikus about elements of nature that you see using a 5 syllable (beat), 7 syllable, 5 syllable sequence.

16. Use toys you find in the car as characters and make up a play or story about them (personification).

17. Make up songs (using familiar tunes) about where you are going, what you are going to do when you get there, how your day has been going so far, etc.

18. Take a journal with you so the kids can draw pictures of things they see from their seats. Later they can add captions to their pictures and eventually use them for story-starters.

19. Play I Spy®.

20. If you are lucky enough to have a portable DVD player, put on a new or unfamiliar movie for the kids and mute the volume. Have them make up the story of what is happening, what the characters' names are, etc.

21. Call out a genre or feeling word or topic and have everyone name as many books as they can that they have read that go along with that word. Then name as many synonyms as you can for the original word.

22. Play 20 questions to practice associations. Think of a famous person and answer yes/no to questions that others

ask about the person until they guess who the person is.

23. Play word-blending games: you say some syllables or sounds and the kids blend them together and tell you the word they make. You can do the same with deletion tasks- taking words apart.

24. Keep magazines in the car for more than reading. Have kids try to find pictures of things you drive by that are also in the magazine.

MATH ACTIVITIES

1. Skip count cars, buildings, etc.

2. Add distances (in miles) between destinations when you are making several stops. Example: It is one mile to the gas station plus three miles to the grocery store plus seven miles to dance class and then nine miles home.

3. Discuss directions (north, south, east, and west) that you are driving to get to a destination.

4. Get in geometry words such as parallel, perpendicular, intersect, and grid by looking at the road.

5. Calculate the miles per gallon your car is getting.

6. Call out shapes of road signs and tally how many of each shape you find.

7. Make a bar graph of different car makes or models. Fill in the graph based on what cars you see on the road as you travel.

The Smart Home

8. Track distance traveled in miles over time at different times of day or on different roads to see which route is fastest, what obstacles slowed you down, how speed affects travel, and so on.

9. Divide your snack up by the time in minutes that you will be away from home to calculate how to ration your food.

10. Add up the receipts from each store you stop at on errand days to see how much Mom and Dad are spending and to keep the family within their budget.

11. Practice auditory math facts: addition, subtraction, multiplication, and division.

12. If the windows are foggy or frosty, kids can work out math problems on them.

13. Tell the kids how far you have traveled and have them tell you how many half miles and quarter miles that translates to be. Then break it down to how many yards, feet, and inches you have gone. You can do the same type of activity with time, calculating how long you have been gone. Translate the hours to partial hours, minutes and seconds.

14. The famous phrase, "Are we there yet?" can get old fast. Give kids an association and understanding of the concept of time by relating quarter and half hours to minutes of a TV show length or something else kids are familiar with. Then tell them how much longer the trip will take in minutes as well as in miles and in "TV show time".

Shannon Pretorius

SOCIAL STUDIES

1. Maps, maps, and more maps! Have kids use a highlighter and chart the route that you take on your way to this place or that each day. See how many different ways you can get to the same place and talk about why they all lead you there.

2. Talk about directions while driving. Have kids use landmarks or the sun to figure out if you are driving north, south, east, or west. They can draw a compass rose on paper and put a checkmark in the direction that you drive to see which direction you drive most often.

3. Infuse vocabulary of landforms such as hill, plateau, plain, mountain, etc. as you drive. Name places you go using landforms that are near it.

4. Going down an unpaved road? Traveling through the country? Making your way through downtown? Use these as opportunities to talk about rural, urban, and suburban areas. Then have kids tell you what kind of an area you are in next time. Use white boards in the car and let them draw some things they would find in each of those areas.

5. Going to be on the road for a while? Relate your car adventure to the adventures of great explorers such as Marco Polo, Christopher Columbus, Lewis and Clark, etc. Talk about how exploring used to be and what it meant to find something or someplace new. (Now get an audio book for the car that goes along with the explorations that you are talking about and experiencing to really make connections!) Ask the kids what types of tools you are

bringing with you for your trip that may have also been used by explorers in the past.

6. Community helpers and organization of a city are wonderful ideas for kids to understand. Have them keep a look out for the police pulling someone over or helping a citizen. Watch for a fire truck passing by to get to an emergency. See how many community helpers or city supports they can point out by the time you get home. Find the buildings those people work in as well.

7. Take a detour to drive past the oldest building in the city or some historic homes in the area. Find the first park to be opened or look for dedications by trees or on buildings. History of where kids live and grow up is right under their noses!

SCIENCE

1. Examine the similarities and differences in structures you pass. How are buildings and cars built differently from one another? How is landscaping arranged to welcome people? Drive through different areas of cities to see how architecture varies from place to place.

2. Force, speed, gears, motion, and machine functions are a few wonderful science topics that go hand-in-hand with cars. Use this vocabulary when kids are asking questions about what makes things go and how things work.

3. When it's raining or the windows fog up or there is frost on the windshield, take the opportunity to talk about water vapor, the water cycle, changes in states of matter, etc.

Jump on any opportunity to show kids in real time what things mean and how they work or how they happen.

4. Get a magnetic board and different kinds of magnets to experiment with in the car.

5. Play meteorologist and predict the weather forecast while making your way through your errands. Then play traffic reporter and do the same with the traffic commute! Making a game out of things like shopping during a storm or waiting in a traffic jam make the situation much more bearable.

6. Experiment with energy while driving. Hypothesize whether driving with the windows down or the heat/air on would take more energy. Why? How about driving with your lights on, or the radio, the air conditioning, or the GPS. See how little and then how much energy you can use at one time in the car and how energy can be saved even there.

7. Electricity is everywhere when you are driving-electrical wires, phone lines, cell phone tower. Discuss how currents work and where electricity comes from and how it works while the kids are looking at the transmitters!

8. With vegetation all around outside those windows, use this time to name different trees, shrubs and flowers. See if the kids can spot them when they come around again.

9. On a sunny, warm day, wrap uncooked s'mores (a graham cracker square with a piece of chocolate and a marshmallow on it and another graham cracker square on

top) in foil. Place them on the seat or in the trunk. When the errands are done, there will be a nice toasty treat waiting for each of you to enjoy.

THE ARTS

1. Listen to music and sing at the top of your lungs! Tap the beat, make up new lyrics, and create car instruments to play using items you find in the car. Make up your own lyrics for tunes with none. Put your hand on your throat and feel the vibrations your voice makes. Sing high and low to see if there is a difference in the vibrations.

2. Make up songs about where you are going. Talk only in song while in the car. Use familiar tunes and change the words to share how your day was, what you are going to be doing while you are out, etc. Some tunes that work well for this are tunes to Mary Had A Little Lamb; The Itsy, Bitsy Spider; Row, Row, Row your Boat; and London Bridge.

3. Keep a drawing pad in the car and draw things you pass by on your daily commute. Sketch something that catches your eye.

4. Color in coloring books for a tranquil, quaint activity, but be careful when keeping crayons in the car. Just as marshmallows will melt, wax will, too!

5. Whistle while you work!

6. Exercise your arms by lifting small hand weights while sitting in the car. Hold your legs together, bend your knees, and lift as high as you can. Repeat 10 times, rest, and try

again. Twist at the waist back and forth for midline exercise.

Travel is a part of our day almost every day, so take advantage of captured time while you can! Everyone has time while they drive somewhere and even more time when they commute by public transportation because the driving is left to someone else. Car-pooling? Great! The more kids the better when it comes to discussions and findings. Not with the kids when you are in the car? Think about some of these things anyway and share your thoughts with them when you get home. Ask them to do the same thing on the school bus the next day and compare notes that evening. What a great way to model and say, "Hey, I am not too old to learn, and I am curious about the world around us, too. I love learning, and I want to share my learning with you." Edu-play is for adults, too!

The Smart Home

ITEMS FOR THE CAR TO ENCOURAGE AN ACTIVE MIND

- Magnetic board with magnet letters and numbers
- Dry erase board and markers
- Maps of the city you live in, cities you visit frequently, and your state
- Highlighters for maps
- A United States map
- Magnetic puzzles
- Travel games such as travel Bingo or tic-tac-toe
- Reading books for the kids
- A nature guide that names local trees, birds, flowers, etc.
- Kid music on CD as well as instrumental music
- Audio books
- Kids' magazines such as *Highlights* or *National Geographic Explorer Kids*
- Healthy snacks
- A personal journal for each child with a pencil and crayons (Don't leave crayons in the car during the summer months.)
- Handheld toys and puppets
- Technology that allows uploads of educational games or

that encourages learning

- Binoculars
- A list of suggested activities for the kids to do in the car (it's hard to think fast while in traffic or after a stressful day when the kids are shouting that they are bored)
- A Rubik's Cube®
- Mad Libs® and a pencil
- Hand puzzles such as brain teasers or square number/picture puzzles
- A calculator to figure out some driving math
- Trivial Pursuit® cards
- Hand weights and an exercise band
- I Spy® books
- Soft instruments
- A water bottle for each person
- Coloring books or sticker books
- Math facts and sight word flashcards
- A deck of cards
- Tracing activities (such as wipe-off placemats)

The Smart Home

- Activity books
- A backpack or organizer to keep materials in
- Magazines to cut apart or tear things out of
- Travel scavenger hunt cards that you make or buy

THE PARENTS' ROLE IN TRAVELING FUN

Some people may have difficulty engaging in some of these activities with kids while driving, but the important thing to remember and focus on is that this is a time when you are contained in a space together and have nowhere else to be. You may have noticed that I did not put headphones on the list of items to have in the car for the kids. Headphones will isolate each child and put them in their own world. They are much less likely to engage and interact with you and others in the car when the headphones go on. They are also less apt to share their ideas, findings, and wonders. Headphones interrupt interaction and communication. The same is true when cell phones are being used.

We have all heard the saying "talk is cheap", but this time it's a good thing. This is a time when you can do something as simple as find out how your child's day was or work out a problem they had at school. Short trip from point A to point B? Great. Give them something to think about (such as some kind of problem or upcoming decision) and let them process through it until you are back in the car together.

Your main job while in the car with the kids is keeping them safe, which means keeping your eyes on the road. There are, however, so many other things we do while driving these days that the list I have created is just a list of sample activities that take little attention and no hands from you. Some can be completed on short trips while others might be better left for longer ones. The idea is again to instill vocabulary, point out the obvious, and relate places, structures, concepts, and environments to your kids' individual lives to make those concepts more meaningful and fun to learn. There doesn't need to be a test or even an assignment. There needs to be constructive, productive conversation, interaction, and mind-stimulating activity that is meaningful, interesting and presented naturally. The more you relate this edu-play to your own life and your kids' lives, the more you will find they are willing and able to participate.

Put the cell phones away. This is not the time to make a quick call while the kids are busy. This is the time for you to listen to them process, problem-solve, think, reflect, and create. It's a time to offer insight, participate in projects, and teach without their even knowing! Any vocabulary you use with them should be in context and come with a short explanation when necessary. Ask open-ended questions that don't have a one word answer and remain interested and excited throughout. Your interest will inspire their interest. Your energy will feed their energy!

CHAPTER GLOSSARY

acrostic - a series of words or phrases written in lines so that the first letter of each line forms a word or saying

alliteration - a string of two or more words that all start with the same consonant(s)

architecture - the character or style of buildings

associations - connections or classifications

author's purpose - the reason the story was written: to entertain, persuade, or inform

auditory - perceived through hearing

bar graph - a graph using parallel bars of varying length to compare amounts

categorize - to arrange in categories or classify by like characteristics

characters - the people or animals who are in a story

coordinates - numbers that define the position of a point

currents - the flow of electrical charge

fluency - read with appropriate pace, intonation, and phrasing

genre - a classification of different types of literature

grid - horizontal and vertical lines that cross at right angles, uniformly spaced, used to plot points

The Smart Home

Haiku - a three-lined Japanese poem about nature that follows the syllable pattern 5-7-5

hypothesis - to make an educated guess using known information

intersect - lines that cross

lyrics - the words to a song

make connections - find a way to connect to the story via personal experiences

parallel - lines running in the same direction that will never meet

perpendicular - lines that cross at a right angle

personification - giving an inanimate object qualities of a person

point of view - the narrator's position

predict - to guess at what will happen

rural - country life or agriculture

setting - where and when the story takes place

states of matter - the forms of solid, liquid, and gas

suburban - pertaining to a sub-urban part of town

summarize - to make a summary; to say what happened in an abbreviated way

syllable - a beat of a word

synonyms - words that mean almost the same thing

Shannon Pretorius

---

tally - a system for recording attempts or numbers

transmitters - the part of a telephone apparatus that converts sound waves into electrical waves

urban - pertaining to living in the city

verse - a part of the song that is not the chorus

water cycle - the natural sequence of water passing through the atmosphere, coming to the ground as a liquid, and then evaporating into the atmosphere again

water vapor - water in the process of evaporation

Chapter 5

Hidden Pictures

Adults see things differently than kids, and truthfully, with the busy, active lives we live today, there are many things that none of us see. We are too busy multi-tasking and rushing and just trying to master the tasks of our day. Not many of us stop to smell the roses anymore, and when we do, we only catch a whiff. This chapter is meant not only to help you stop and notice the world around you, but to help teach kids the importance of and pleasure in noticing and appreciating the little things in life.

Vocabulary Words You Might Find When You Play

shapes, lines, curves, angles, colors, edges, length, random, tessellation, pattern, rotate, reflect, variety, segment, parallel, perpendicular, point, intersect, position, purpose, polygon, open shape, closed shape, roll

Shannon Pretorius

WHAT'S HIDING IN YOUR PATH?

1. Kids, sit in your favorite room in your house and look around. See how many different shapes you can find when you look at each of the objects that are in there. Close one eye and use your finger tip to trace the shape from where you are sitting. Can you name the shape? Is it a polygon? Is it an open shape or a closed shape? You might want to do this in your bedroom when you are trying to fall asleep at night. Now draw the shape on paper and see if it tessellates. (Don't do this at bedtime though.) That is, see if you can put copies of the shape next to each other without leaving spaces between the lines of the shape. A square tessellates, a trapezoid does, too. If the shape you are working with does not tessellate, can you add another shape to it that is in the room and tessellate the two together? See what kind of drawing you can come up with when doing this. Where did you find the shape? Why was the shape there? Is it a decoration? Does the shape serve a purpose? Could a different shape be used there?

2. Solids have a defined shape; liquids take on the shape of their container. Some shapes are obvious and others don't really show up unless you are looking for them. Some of them you can name, and others don't really resemble anything you know a name for. Kids, take a walk (inside or out) and tally on a chart what kinds of shapes you see. Have a spot for polygons or regular shapes, have another spot for open shapes or shapes that don't seem to have an end, and have another spot to tally shapes that are part of other shapes. For example, a door is a rectangle and there may be smaller rectangles on it, and there may be a rhombus on each side of the smaller rectangles. There could be a circle door knob and circular screws and cylindrical and rectangle hinges. So many shapes on one door! The purpose here is to notice details, to see

The Smart Home

how things are put together, and to see how shapes are used in everyday objects.

3. How many intersections are in your house? Intersections aren't just for roads or grids. They are found at any place where two paths cross. Do the intersections in your house meet at right angles? Do they cross or just meet? Travel the path of one floor in your house, noticing the intersections and what creates them. Are they made by walls, by furniture arrangement, or by flooring? What kind of angles do the lines of intersection form? Acute, obtuse, right, or straight?

4. Find some wood in your house. Wood grain is a great place to find hidden pictures. Use your imagination, follow the swirls, and see what shapes or pictures you can make out of the grain in the wood. Make up a story about the patterns or pictures of the wood on the cupboards, wood of the office desk, or the patterns of the wood floor. Are all of the woods the same? How are they different from one another? Can you figure out what kind of tree the wood came from? Can you see knots in the wood? Is the wood "hard" or "soft"? Was the tree deciduous or coniferous? Answering these questions can give you a greater appreciation for how we use natural elements every day.

5. The clouds are always moving and changing. If you have some kind of lava lamp or similar toy at home, the shapes in that may always be changing as well. When you turn on a lamp in your bedroom at night, it creates pictures on the wall also. We can find pictures and shapes in so many objects that are around us every day. Cloud watching is a fun activity. See what kinds of shapes or images you can see in the clouds. Make up a story using all the different images you perceive. This is a relaxing activity that is

great for one person, two, or the whole family. Each person sees things from a different perspective, so the stories that develop will be interesting every time.

6. A shadow is caused by light being blocked by a solid opaque object (such as your hand). Shadow puppets are fun to make, easy to change, and wonderful to tell stories with. Use a lamp in a dark room, a flashlight on a dark wall, or an overhead projector on a blank wall to create your playground. Now use your hands, in different combinations, to make characters. Have one person put a piece of paper on the wall and trace the character you have created. Now give the character a name, a personality, a voice, and tell a story about it. Change your hand position and create a new character and do the same thing again. Not into story-telling? Make objects with your hands instead of characters and have others guess what object you have created or make scenery that goes together. Using the light and your hands, you can create just about anything you imagine. Put your hands together with someone else to make bigger designs. This is a great evening edu-play activity for families.

The great thing about hidden pictures and finding shapes, lines, numbers, pictures, etc. hidden in every day objects is that your eyes and your mind are working together. Start with these simple ideas and let your eyes pull you in different directions while your mind jumps on board with new ways of looking at old things. See if you can make new the old things that you have been looking at daily for years!

The Smart Home

OBJECTS OR PLACES THAT HAVE MANY HIDDEN PICTURES

- Wood of all kinds-the grainier the better
- Fabrics on chairs or couches
- Wallpaper
- Rugs, tapestries, or linoleum flooring
- Bedding
- Big trees/flowers
- The garden
- The spinning washer
- Windows (especially dirty ones) and window frames or doors
- Computer screen savers
- A darkened room at dusk or dawn
- Sidewalks and roads (safety first)
- Bike frames
- Anything outside on a windy day
- The inside of a car, bus, train, or subway
- The outside of a house

- Road signs
- Book covers
- The park
- A swing set
- Artwork
- Water-the pool, the lake, the river, the bathtub…
- Magazine pictures
- The beach or sand box
- A fireplace or fire pit
- Ropes, chains, fences, etc.
- Sculptures
- Cursive handwriting
- People and animals
- A garage or basement or attic
- Any store
- The refrigerator (just don't leave it opened for too long)
- The grocery cart
- A calendar

The Smart Home

THE PARENTS' ROLE IN BRINGING THINGS OUT OF HIDING

Some people are naturally observant and can describe in great detail what they saw on their way to work, school, home, etc. Other people have an artistic eye that moves directly to lines, colors, organization or shape of objects, and to the flow of objects or scenery around them. Still others of us don't have either of these natural abilities. All of us often miss out on so much that goes on in the world around us. What's important about this chapter is for kids to take time to notice the little things--the details that make up the bigger picture. When we write narratives, details create images in the readers' minds. When we describe a place or object to a person to heighten their understanding, details make all the difference. When we do a presentation, the details we put into it are what make it outstanding. When we read instructions or clean the house or do homework or make a fabulous meal, call the doctor for test results, it's the details that are important. In a fast paced world, details are easily lost and the quick version, the big picture, is what people are looking for. That's why this chapter breaks down the big picture to remind us of the little things.

How often do you look forward to waiting in line or waiting at the doctor's office or waiting on hold for the next available representative? You just can't wait until you have to do it again, right? How many other things do you try to quickly accomplish while you are waiting? Return some e-mails, go through the mail, update your calendar, quickly help Johnny finish his math homework, start dinner, etc. How quickly does your patience leave you? How irritated do you get while having to wait? How about using that time that always creeps into our day somewhere (even waiting for the elevator to reach your floor) to find pictures and shapes hidden in the environment that surrounds you. Be excited about the time that you wait somewhere or for something. Show your kids what you see and ask them what they see before you hear the dreaded "How much longer?" or "This is so boring!" that will soon leak from their mouths. Patience is a virtue!

Leading by example: I can't impress upon you how important this concept is. Challenge yourself and your kids to find shapes, lines, pictures, or patterns in bigger items everywhere you go. Your job is to teach your kids how to use their time and what they can do with it. The edu-play presented in this chapter teaches you what to do with the empty space in your day. These are the times when you feel trapped because you are waiting. You aren't trapped, you are in luck! Use the activities suggested to start your family on a journey that will open your eyes to so many things that you never noticed before. These are also great ways to enhance the story-telling and imaginations of your children.

Point of view: Everyone sees things differently. Try taking on your kids' point of view when they are showing you what they see in that old deck board or on the butterfly's wing. What's new is exciting and what's exciting is finding something new to share together. Enjoy yourself and let your mind go crazy...in a good way.

The Smart Home

CHAPTER GLOSSARY

acute angle - an angle measuring smaller than 90 degrees

angles - the space within two lines that meet at a point

categorize - to place in categories with similarities

closed shape - a shape whose sides all connect, leaving no opening

coniferous - evergreen trees or shrubs

cylindrical - having the form of a cylinder (like a can)

deciduous - trees and shrubs that shed their leaves annually

intersection - where two lines cross

obtuse angle - an angle measuring between 91 and 179 degrees- greater than a right angle

opaque - not allowing light to pass through

opened shape - a shape whose sides do not all connect

polygon - a closed figure, having three or more sides that are usually straight lines

regular polygon - a closed shape with all sides and angles being of equal measure

rhombus - an equilateral parallelogram

right angle - an angle measuring 90 degrees (and forming an L)

rotate - to turn on an axis or center point

straight angle - an angle measuring 180 degrees or a straight line

tessellate - form or arrange shapes in a checkerboard or mosaic pattern

transformations - to change in form or appearance

trapezoid - a 4-sided shape having two parallel and two non-parallel sides

CHAPTER 6

READING BETWEEN THE LINES

We all know that reading is important and that reading to our kids is vital. Because we know that, we intentionally fit it into our daily (or weekly) routines. Reading to kids at bedtime seems to be a popular choice, and a great way for them to wind down before hitting the pillow. Some kids are avid readers and want to read every chance they get while others don't think taking time to read is an enjoyable family activity. When you have two or more kids, sometimes it's hard to find books that will suit each child's taste and comprehension level. That may deter you from reading together. Hopefully this chapter will help you find other ways to encourage and foster reading when you can't always sit down with a book.

Vocabulary to Read About

characters, setting, mood, theme, plot, conflict, problem, solution, moral, informational, narrative, expository, persuasive, main idea, details, cause and effect, point of view, author's purpose, fact and opinion, conclusions, inference, predict, text features, text connections, story line

Shannon Pretorius

ENCOURAGING READING

1. Using reading vocabulary in context in order to help kids understand the idea behind reading (more than just saying the words) can be just as powerful as reading itself. When asking your children about their day, ask questions about a specific topic. For example, you can ask who they played with at recess (the characters), where they played (setting), and what equipment they used or games they played. You can ask whether there were any conflicts, and if so, what solutions they came up with. Finally, ask how things went, and what the mood was when they got back inside from recess. Now I know that many kids won't take the time to humor you and answer all those questions, or the answers will quickly become "I don't know," so just take note of what they do tell you. You can summarize for them what you understood from the information that they did give you and tell it back to them like a story. Then maybe they will fill in the missing pieces for you in order to correct any errors you made. You could also change some of the questions into yes/no questions that might be easier for younger kids to answer, or less annoying to kids who are impatient with questioning. Predicting what will happen tomorrow at recess given how today ended would also be a possibility here. Then tomorrow, check your predictions with a follow-up conversation. You could use this strategy with any part of your child's day. The more they hear the words, the better connection they will make to the vocabulary. This is also a great activity for showing how important active listening is to comprehension and communication.

2. Actions have consequences (whether positive or negative) and causes have effects. When correcting behavior, focusing attention on something, or sharing about your day, use these words

and show their relationship to each other. Share how the cause of running errands and cleaning on Saturday leads to the effect of fun time on Sunday. The cause of not getting the garbage container to the curb on time for garbage day leads to the effect of having a smelly garage for the week. This works very well in nature. The cause and effect of rain or lack of rain, heavy storms, wind, and also too much heat are relationships that kids can experience everyday. Using these words not only helps kids understand relationships of this manner, but it also helps them think about their own actions and the reactions that occur because of their actions.

3. Kids exaggerate often (and admit it; adults can tell a story or two themselves), so take advantage of these times by introducing the concepts of fact and opinion and point of view. Listen to two people rehash an event that occurred and point out the differences in their stories. Few stories will be retold exactly the same way because of the point of view of each person watching it all unfold. Different points of view are one reason arguments take place. Next time your kids are arguing, challenge them to see the situation through the other person's point of view. Fact and opinion work in a similar fashion. Exaggeration might lead to a fact being stretched just enough that it isn't really a fact anymore. One person's opinion may clash with another person's opinion and cause a disagreement among friends or siblings (or between parents for that matter). Introduce these words, their meanings, and point out ways they are used. Then relate these ideas to stories that you read with your kids.

4. Are you really playing that board game or card game by the rules? Do you use all the features on your television, oven, cell phone, DVR, etc.? Do your kids read the directions for playing their video games? Do you follow recipes when cooking? What a great

way to practice informational reading-manuals are everywhere! This will also work for some toys, such as Lego® sets that come with step-by-step directions. And speaking of directions, how about following directions to a friend's house or to a location you have never been? Informational reading opportunities surround us every day. Write up your own family rule book, procedure pamphlet, or chore directions with the help of the family!

5. Being persuasive is a talent that comes naturally to some people while others spend their lives trying to develop it as a skill! When the "What's for lunch?" question arises and the answer is met with a strong groan, allow your kids to get an argument together that will persuade you to change the menu to a second option of *your* choice. Working on persuasive arguments will help them understand the same concept in reading. (Beware; this will also come in handy when they are teenagers trying to get you to lend them the car for the night!) If you have more flexibility, try this same idea with dinner. Boy would the kids feel like winners then!

6. Main idea and details are at the heart of many texts. Bring these concepts to life while asking kids about their day, (having them tell you the events backwards might be easier since they are starting with the most recent event first), helping them study for their history test, or discussing your last vacation. Strike up a conversation with the kids about a vacation you all took together. Ask them what they remember about it. If it was some time ago, or if they didn't enjoy it, they may offer very few memories of the occasion. Get out the photo album and look through the evidence of what happened on that trip. Point out that they remembered the main idea (where you went, one specific thing you did while there…), but that some of the details were left out. "We did go to

Grandma's house and she did make burnt cookies, but did you forget about trying to choke down the cookies with milk and finding that the milk you were chugging was spoiled? And what about the pan that had to be scrubbed for three days before the charred pieces of cookie would come off?" These are details that make the main event even more memorable. Once you describe a few details, the kids will start remembering even more. And of course their point of view of the vacation will be interesting, too! Sally may be sure that Johnny fell in love with the neighbor, Pam, while Johnny insists he was way too busy to have time for Pam and never even noticed her while they were there. Using transition words is another skill that will come into play naturally here. (First, next, then, after that, finally, before, during...)

7. Our lives are a living, breathing book that just hasn't been written. Use that idea to infuse predicting, story line and text connections into your thoughts and conversations. What do the kids think the day will bring? What will they do at school that day? What do they want their story line to look like? Create a story board together using blank index cards or whatever other tools you have handy. Have kids draw out the story of their day, week, or their lives (past, present, or future) in pictures. These would be great items to keep in their memory book or hope chest to bring out and show them when they are older. Also, as events happen throughout the week, make connections to movies, books, or situations that happened to others you know that are similar to what is happening to you or your child. Use phrases such as, "This reminds me of a situation in a book I read about..." or "This reminds me of a time when...". Making these connections while reading is important for enhancing comprehension of the text, so introducing them and practicing them in life situations will help them become

second nature when reading.

Reading at any age and stage is extremely important, and opportunities for reading can be found everywhere. Hopefully the ideas presented here will encourage you to think beyond only book reading or bedtime reading and help you soak up all the opportunities that are available to you and your kids as you trek through your days.

The Smart Home

READING STRATEGY QUESTIONS AND STATEMENTS THAT CAN BE USED ANYTIME

- Based on what you just saw, what do you think will happen next?

- How do you suppose that person felt when that happened to them?

- Can you think of a time that you felt that same way?

- This incident reminds me of ...

- How did that situation turn out in the end?

- I understand that the main point was ___, but can you remind me of some of the details or specifics that took place?

- I wonder...

- We may just be able to do that IF you can persuade me to do so.

- Tell me three facts you learned today.

- What is your opinion about that?

- What was the cause of that?

- How did that action affect you? Others around you?

- That phone call changed my mood.

- I see there is a conflict here. What solution can you come up with to resolve this?

- The moral of this story is…
- The purpose of this conversation is…
- What events in your life can you think of that are similar to this?
- If you could change the ending to your day, what would be different?
- How did that event change you?
- Describe that place to me so I can picture it in my head, too.
- I see that you and I have different points of view on that topic.
- My purpose for saying that is…
- Let's look that up to find out more about it.

THE PARENTS' ROLE - YOU ARE PRACTICING IT HERE!

The goal for this chapter is to infuse reading vocabulary into the ever developing story of your lives. You and your kids are creating your own personal narrative as you journey through life, experiencing all the new and exciting chapters that present themselves. In a way, life is like one of those Choose Your Own Adventure Books® that were around when I was a kid. The first part of the story is laid out for you, but then you get to a point where it is up to you to decide what comes next. If you choose path A, then B will happen. If you choose path N, then Z will happen. As you maneuver through the days, weeks, months, and years that suddenly leave a trail of life behind you, interact with your life story in the same way you would interact with a book. Discuss it, reflect on it, get lost in it, cherish it, and use reading vocabulary to help make sense of the voyage.

There are so many reading opportunities that arise each day. To immerse your kids in reading more often than at bedtime, try some of these suggestions:

1. Turn on the closed-captioning feature on the television.

2. Send them a text or an e-mail just for fun.

3. Have them read you the recipe you are working on from the cook book.

4. Read the newspaper together instead of watching or listening to the news.

5. Subscribe to a magazine for kids such as *National Geographic Kids*, *Highlights*, *High Five*, or *Discovery Kids*.

6. Kids love to get mail. Encourage them to start sending pen pal letters to friends in the neighborhood (to save on stamp costs) or to relatives their age. They will love reading the letters they get in return!

7. Put the cereal box in front of them as they eat breakfast.

8. Have them read labels when grocery shopping with you. Give them a certain ingredient or nutrition fact to look for.

9. Get them on reading websites such as *PBSKids.org*, or *StarFall.com*. (There are many others out there as well.) The public library is a great place to do this for free.

10. Read signs and billboards aloud as you drive, bike, or ride the bus together.

Kids learn from their parents. Do your kids ever see you read? Make a point to talk about what YOU are reading, whether it be a book for enjoyment, a work-related article, the minutes from a meeting, or a magazine. Of course all content is not appropriate for kids, so no juicy details are necessary, but let them know what it is, why you are reading it, and what you learned from it. And, of course, we don't all enjoy everything we have to read, so no need to sugar coat it. It's OK to acknowledge that you find some of your work articles boring, or that you have a hard time connecting to a particular article in the paper because you have limited background knowledge of the situation. When kids understand these issues, they may better appreciate the many purposes and types of reading we engage in, and you could be helping them cope with difficulties they are having with their own reading.

CHAPTER GLOSSARY

cause - events that make other events happen

characters - the people or animals that are in a story

comprehension - understanding intended meaning

conflicts - problems

context - statements in a book that often clarify meaning

details - all the information that supports the main idea

effect - what happens as the result of an event

expository - non-fiction writing

fact - something that can be proven

fiction - made up; note real

informational reading - true stories meant to provide information about a topic to the reader

main idea - the primary focus of a writing

mood - the feeling of a piece of writing

opinion - someone's feeling about an issue that can not be proven

persuasive - convincing others of your beliefs or point of view

point of view - the way a person sees an event; one person's perception

predict - a guess at what will happen next/later in the story

setting - where and when a story takes place

summarize - to sum up what happened in a story

story line - the plot

text connections - having a similar experience to a story and using that experience to help you understand the story

Chapter 7

Yeah Write, Mom!

Good old fashion writing seems to be becoming a thing of the past. How often do we pick up a pencil and piece of paper and just write? I make my grocery lists and to-do lists on paper; I write in my daughter's journal the old fashioned way; I still write in greeting cards by hand; and in photo album comment boxes; but that's about where it ends. Many people don't even write checks anymore! Even this book was conceived on a computer, instead of on reams of paper. The good news is that we are communicating more in writing in other ways through texting and e-mailing and blogging and chatting and instant messaging and updating statuses, all using technology. We used to use the telephone to get a message to someone. Now we have a number of written ways to contact people instead. So, although the art of handwriting is fighting to hold on, the poetry of writing itself is still alive and well.

This chapter is about encouraging and fostering the art of writing without making it a chore. Look for places to enhance writing that is already taking place, encourage opportunities that are not being taken advantage of at this time, and, of course, embed this edu-play naturally into everyday routines!

Writing Increases Expressive Vocabulary!

brainstorm, draft, revise, edit, publish, story, insert, main idea, details, illustrations, purpose, topic, communicate, ideas, journaling, lists, compose, format, message, inform, entertain

WRITE ON!

1. Young kids love to act things out or take on roles of adults. You can encourage this edu-play by incorporating writing at the same time. Let your children take charge of dinner by playing restaurant. They can write up a menu, including writing an introduction to their restaurant, and create a catchy advertisement for the front of the menu. Then they can write your order on a notepad and even write up a bill for you when the meal is through.

2. Does your son or daughter really want to go to a movie that just came out or get you to drive him/her around town with a friend? Does your youngest want ice cream for dessert tonight? Encourage them to stop nagging you and to design a poster that will persuade you instead. What better way to get someone's attention than through advertising! They could also write a commercial or a skit and then perform it for you if that seems more fun. Whatever the method, let the good times roll! By the way, this will help keep them occupied in a productive way while you take that power nap on the couch or finish a task you haven't had time for.

3. E-mailing or texting can at times be a more productive way to communicate with your preteen than face-to-face talking when you are (momentarily) so "un-cool" to them. Ask them what their plans are for the afternoon, what they would like for dinner, or what homework they have through a text message or e-mail. If they don't respond, go bug them in person. That may encourage them to answer in writing the next time, and if not, you just had some great one-on-one time together. Once you have a solid e-mail rapport, ask them for details such as who will be there, what time they will be home, what the requirements of their homework

assignment are, when it is due, etc.

4. Ask your kids to make lists to help you to keep up with them: school items they are out of, projects they are supposed to be working on, grocery wishes, gift lists, schedule of weekend activities, and things they want to do. Lists are one way to get ideas down in a productive manner and teach them about the organization of ideas, and the chunking of common items. White boards hung at kid height work well for this.

5. Journaling is a fantastic, personal way to reflect, to jot down ideas, and to express oneself without the criticism of others. Journaling can start at any age, and ideas can be expressed through words or through pictures. Journaling could become part of a nighttime routine, part of Saturday morning quiet time, or be an activity for the car. For jotting down thoughts anytime, try hanging white boards at kid height. Whatever time is used, journaling is a great way to articulate ideas, express oneself, and work out feelings. Adults can journal with their kids too. Keep a journal about your kids to show them when they are grown. Journal your family's dietary habits, favorite foods, games, outings or traditions, daily feelings, wishes for the future…the possibilities are endless! Journals are also great items to pack when going on vacation. Each person can keep a log of the vacation as they live it from their own point of view. What a treat to review those journals or logs together a year or two later, reliving special experiences through the varied lenses of multiple family members.

6. Poetry is often interesting to kids because of its rhythmic and rhyming verse and because of the fun you can have with the words. Dr. Seuss is the master, but your child can be pretty good at it, too. Start with some rhyming in the bathtub or at the dinner table. Brainstorm ideas for words that rhyme with something you are eating or something in the room. Then discuss things you know about that item and draft a short poem about it. Each person involved can be challenged to come up with one line for the poem. It can be silly, imaginative, real, accurate, and can even include made-up words that are understandable by the context in which they are used. Do you know what a "drogam" is? Can you imagine what it is if I say, "The 'drogam' worked like a charm and put everyone to sleep."? As the author, the choice of words and how to use them is all yours. Once someone has written everyone's ideas on paper, revise the lines to pull them together, edit the content, and then publish your piece by hanging it on the fridge to share with everyone. This idea of shared poetry and walking through the writing process together would also work well for working through arguments, disagreements, or issues among the kids and their siblings or friends.

Writing is an art, whether accomplished through the latest technology or by simply using the chicken scratch method; whether it involves paragraphs, stories, and books or simply words, lists, and sentences. Use the edu-play presented here to take the mystery and anxiety out of the art of writing and show the brilliant pieces that can emerge from the drawing on a napkin or the doodling on the frosty car window.

The Smart Home

QUICK WRITES AND ENCOURAGING WRITING

- Use the shower steam on the mirror to leave a message for the person waiting in line for the bathroom.

- Have a message board (wipe-off board) hanging in the bathroom. You would be amazed at how many ideas and thoughts start there!

- Leave note pads or sticky pads all over the house with pencils attached. Doodles soon turn into characters and story lines.

- Put a note in your child's lunch box or backpack. Then leave your purse, briefcase, backpack, etc. out for them to respond.

- Write in code with your kids. Make up your own code and send secret messages to them (or have them do this with friends).

- Get bath crayons or shower crayons and allow them to be used!

- Start a family blog and let everyone make entries.

- Anger is a hard feeling for kids to understand and cope with. Journaling is a great way to express oneself without hurting the feelings of others.

- Write a family newsletter containing articles that name accomplishments of each person's month. Everyone can author one article. The newsletter can also include classified and want ads! Hang it on the refrigerator or send it to grandma and grandpa to keep them up-to-date on what is happening with your family.

- Lists and menu options are endless. One person can write the dinner menu for the week and the other can make the grocery list from that. Someone else can write out the chores list and another person can update the calendar for the week, listing everyone's activities, assignments, appointments, etc.

- Pen pals are a wonderful way to get kids writing and interacting with others. Use old babysitters, family members, neighbors, friends of friends, mentors, etc.

- Buy postcards when you visit somewhere and have the kids send them home to themselves, to a relative, to you, or back to the person you are visiting as a thank you.

- Write a new end to a favorite story or add a new character to the mix.

- Write song lyrics to a familiar tune.

- Write a set of rules for your home (and rules for little brother in your bedroom).

- Cut out stars from plain paper and write wishes (personal goals) for the week/month and post them somewhere. Celebrate when they are achieved.

- Write in the sand outside with a stick or with chalk on the sidewalk.

- Write directions to lead someone somewhere and see if

they can find their way.

- Write thank you messages.

- Host a day of silence (more like an hour). *Write* all necessary communication to each other.

- Write captions on the backs of pictures.

- Write lists of rhyming words.

- Make up new words and write pretend definitions for them and then use them in sentences.

- Use old magazine pictures to write stories. Cut them out and add captions or speech/thought bubbles to the people. Arrange them on paper with cut scenery to create your own comic or narrative.

WRITE ON, PARENTS!

Again, just like in the other chapters, your job is as a coach and facilitator, encouraging discovery, growth, and new ideas. You may find that your involvement and participation are needed more here than in pursuing ideas presented in other chapters. The complexity of written expression and the difficulty of developing ideas can be challenging and time-consuming. As time goes on, however, as the kids gain more experience, they will eventually just take over. Like any chapter in this book, these activity ideas and leads are only going to go as far as you take them. Your excitement, encouragement, enjoyment, and energy will go a long way in the development of new habits and discovery of new passions. It seems that kids these days have less time to explore new ideas that are not part of their basic daily "must". We do what we do and we know what we know and we move from week to week that way. You can help push the exploration of new territory and encourage the curiosity that comes naturally to kids.

Kids learn by example and tend to follow in their parents' footsteps. They are more likely to do things that they see you doing (unless they are teenagers, of course). Only have one computer? Set up a calendar and time slots for different people to use it. Don't want to spend money on journals that you don't think will be used? Make some by stapling folded paper together and letting the kids design their own covers. Use pieces of a brown paper bag as the front and back cover for more protection of the pages.

Most importantly, use new language, don't be afraid of exploring writing in a new, unfamiliar way, and be patient. New skills don't always form naturally or quickly. Use some of the vocabulary that accompanies writing for a while. Then do some

The Smart Home

oral story telling or writing activities together. When you think it's time, try one new idea and let your kids get used to it for a while. Give it time to take hold. If it isn't a good fit, try something else. Don't overwhelm yourself or your children by bombarding them with too many choices at one time.

If you can, keep track somehow of what you have tried, how it went, and of course keep track of new ways of edu-playing when they arise. Since the ideas that I give you here are just the tip of the iceberg, you will undoubtedly come up with others that are not mentioned. Add them to your list! The more items you keep in your bag of tricks, the more avenues you have to encourage a healthy, active mind and spirit in your children.

Chapter Glossary

articulate - to express your meaning

brainstorm - to come up with ideas related to a topic before writing

chunking - to break into manageable pieces or pieces that have similar characteristics

draft - to jot down your ideas in sentence form

edit - to correct grammar and spelling errors

inform - to provide information to someone on a given topic

journaling - writing down your thoughts

persuade - to convince

publish - to make a piece of writing available for others to read

revise - to make changes to a piece of writing

writing process - the steps taken to complete a written piece

CHAPTER 8

SO MUCH TO DO; SO LITTLE TIME!

This chapter is dedicated to the parents of children who don't understand the concept of time, don't care about the concept of time, don't know how to tell time, or who are always just taking their time. Whether we like it or not, our lives seem to revolve around time. For some it is an organizational wonder, while for others it is a curse.

This chapter is composed of a variety of ideas for helping kids (and maybe yourself) appreciate, value, or in the least, pay attention to time. Busy lives necessitate some kind of schedule and chances are you have a good one going. These tips may just make it a little more fun.

WARNING: WE ALL LOSE TRACK OF TIME OR FOR ONE REASON OR ANOTHER HAVE TO HURRY SOMETIMES. HURRYING CAN LEAD TO CARELESSNESS. PLEASE DO NOT COMPROMISE YOUR WITS, YOUR DRIVING SKILLS, OR SAFETY WHEN WORKING ON TIME AND HURRYING ALONG. IT'S BETTER TO STOP TO MAKE SURE THE COFFEE POT IS OFF OR THE DOOR IS LOCKED THEN TO RUSH OUT THE DOOR WITH 10 SECONDS TO SPARE!

Time for Some Relevant Vocabulary!

hour, half hour, quarter to/quarter past, half past, digital, analog, second, minute, clockwise, counterclockwise

Shannon Pretorius

TIME TO SHARE IDEAS

1. Let kids feel how long a minute really is. Set a timer for one minute and have them do nothing for that time-not even talk. Then do it again, but this time have them try to get as much done as they possibly can. (I wouldn't suggest inhaling as much food as possible, but they could try to get dressed, make their beds or pack their lunches.) The minute they used for the first part of the activity will surely feel much longer than the second! Have some play dough around? Have one person make an object for one minute. Then the next person has one minute to add to it or change it in some way. Continue play until each person has had a turn. Compare the beginning object to the end result when transformations are complete. Play around with minutes a bit more as you go through your day. Keep track of how many minutes it takes to get to school, how many minutes a commercial break is on television, how many minutes it takes for your bread to pop out of the toaster. Using a stop watch, digital timer, or a clock with a second hand will work well for these activities. Whatever you have available is fine. Counting 1 Mississippi 2 Mississippi also works! Once the concept of a minute is understood, have your kids use timers or a clock to carefully calculate how many minutes it takes them to do each part of their morning or daily routine. How long does it take to get dressed or to brush their teeth? This will help assure that they have enough time to comfortably achieve their morning goals before leaving the house.

2. Show kids what a certain time looks like on the clock. For example, if you want them to do homework for one hour, show them what that looks like on the clock. Then leave the clock in front of them while they work through their tasks. This will help avoid the "Am I done yet?!?!" whining and inquiries. You can also

relate this amount of time to something they know. "You will be reading for the time it takes to watch one (insert favorite show here)." Or, "We will leave for the bus stop in 10 minutes, which is how long it takes for your eggs to boil." Giving kids a time warning or notice is easier and more effective when they have a known, comfortable time framework to relate to, and will help them understand just how long (or short) that time really is.

3. If you are struggling to get your kids out of the house in the morning, in from the backyard for dinner, or out of the bathtub in the evening, create a visual schedule together that will help them see the things they will be able to do with their time. Break the time down together and ask them what they need or want to accomplish with their time. Then write it down on a schedule for them to reference during that activity time. This will save you from having to nag them every three minutes so they move on to the next task. If they are really struggling, set a timer to beep when the time for each activity is done. Then the schedule is the guide, not you!

4. Kids love to win. They will make anything into a race just so they can win. Some things, like eating, brushing teeth, and completing homework assignments should not be a race, but if you are having difficulty getting your kids to complete other jobs on time, give them a piece of paper and have them start timing themselves, writing down the time it takes them to complete an assigned task. Then they can set a goal to try to show improvement each day or each week. It's a race against time!

5. If your kids aren't listening to you when you tell them they need to be in the car or at the table in a certain amount of minutes, try telling them in a different way. Instead of letting them know

the car is leaving in 15 minutes, tell older kids they have a quarter of an hour. Hearing the time this way will cause them to consciously process what you said. "Dinner will be put away at half past 7. You have until then to eat." Are your little ones begging you to let them stay up later? Tell them their bedtime in minutes or seconds. Let them decide what time they go to bed. "You can stay up for 10 more minutes, one sixth of an hour, or 600 more seconds. It's your choice."

6. How often do parents tell their kids that it's time for *something*? "Time to go." "Time for bed." "Time to turn off the computer." How often do kids listen to that the first time? Use time more specifically to explain yourself, or at least to give kids a more thorough description of this time. "It's 8:30, which is bed time!" "Your video game has been running for 30 minutes, which is all we allow." "It's 7:00 now, which is when you take a bath on school nights." For some kids (and some parents) this will take time to work. For others, this simple change in vocabulary may be all it takes to achieve immediate cooperation.

The Smart Home

TIME FOR SOME FUN

- Make clocks using paper plates, cardboard for the hands, and a brad in the center to hold the pieces together.

- Teach time using whole fruit to represent an hour and its cut segments to represent portions of an hour.

- Play games that use timers (sand timers work too) such as Boggle®, Topple®, etc.

- Create visual schedules for necessary tasks with their times next to them.

- Bake or cook together, showing how important the concept of time is when it comes to cooking.

- When preparing for a big meal, encourage the kids to list each step in the preparation along with the time it will take to accomplish that step. A fun (and useful) exercise is to count back from dinner time, listing each step in the process similar to a space lift off countdown. "At T minus 5, we wash our hands for dinner; at T minus 10, the rolls go into the oven to warm; at T minus 20, we set the table; at T minus 45, the potatoes go into the oven."

- Track time while exercising together.

- Cover all the clocks for one day and tell time using feelings of hunger, feeling tired, etc. and by tracking the sun.

- Time different activities you complete and see if you can improve your time. Puzzle cubes, brain teasers, or other puzzles are good to use here.

- Play games where you do things in slow motion or in fast forward motion. Fast forward play will also come in handy to use when you are running late and will avoid putting stress on the kids if they are used to it being a game.

- Plan obstacle courses and then race through them, trying to improve your time with each attempt.

- Spend more time having family time!

- Combine activities to open up more time for desired tasks. This is a great way to teach kids about multi-tasking.

- Help the kids document each thing they do each day and how long each activity takes. Then organize the tasks from the smallest amount of time to the greatest. Are the results surprising? Once they see this, they may want to make some changes!

- Use only military time for a day or a week.

- At dinner, pose the question, "What if each day had ___ hours in it?" Each person can share what they would want to do with the extra time, or what they would cut out if the day was made shorter.

- Make a list of things you would like to spend more time doing and find the time in your week to do them.

- Make YOU time! Create "dance time", "reading time" or some other activity time for your family. Whenever someone yells "___ time!" everyone has to stop what they are doing and participate for a designated amount of time.

- Take your time! Forget the rush for one day and just enjoy free time.

- Forbid the word "time" from the family's vocabulary for a day.

THE PARENTS' ROLE THIS TIME

Of course it's your job to keep things moving and to get yourself through each day. We often get so busy with what we are doing that we are racing against time and it becomes our enemy instead of being a tool to help us. If you find you are cursing the clock, it's time to stop and change things. We will never have enough time in our day to accomplish everything. That's why I have written this book about edu-playing. I don't want to add more to your plate, but rather alter the way you or your kids are doing things to allow for an infusion of educational talk and play while you make your way through each day. With the ideas presented in this chapter, your challenge is to teach the concept of time in a way that works for you. Think about how you use time each day, what it means to you and then teach your kids. Do they need to know the times that things will be happening that day? Maybe they need to be taught how to tell time. Whatever their understanding of time is, use that to teach them the skill of managing time, using time to their advantage, and of course, the importance of time when there are deadlines, events to get to, or when they are wasting the time of others!

I love the phrase "make time for that". I wish I could make time for everything. See how you and your family can organize your day smarter instead of always trying to make time for something else. Can you double up on things by doing homework on the long drive home? Can you have the kids bathe while you are preparing dinner? Use time to your advantage. If you make it a challenge and let kids in on the plan, they will enjoy racing against time in order to complete whatever activities need completing. Prioritizing what is to be completed in a day will also help.

Use time well. We all have the same twenty-four hours to use each day, but how we use those hours can make a huge difference in the quality of our days. Are there regular moments, times of day, or activities that habitually seem stressful for a lack of time? Is morning always feeling rushed? Are you constantly nagging your five-year-old to eat breakfast a little faster, to be quicker in getting dressed, to quit dawdling while brushing her teeth? Do you tend to be stressed while you're driving because you're always running five minutes late? Do you hate always racing to get to work on time, to pick up the kids from school or day care on time, to reach the dry cleaner before it closes, and so on? If you are plagued with time-connected stress, it's time to reorganize your day.

Getting up earlier may sound dreadful, but an extra ten or fifteen minutes in the morning may dramatically change the tenor of the morning experience for you AND for your children. Recognizing you are typically running late means you need to allow an extra ten minutes or so to reach your destination. "It's only a five-minute drive" may be true, but realize that it will take you another five minutes to leave your house or office, get into your car, and actually be on your way. Pay attention to your gas tank as well as a last-minute fill-up can demand significantly extra time.

CHAPTER GLOSSARY

analog - time represented mechanically using hands on a (usually) round clock

clockwise - moving around a clock in the direction that the numbers go-to the right from the top

counterclockwise - moving toward the left from the top, the opposite way that the numbers run on a clock

digital - time represented on a clock in numerical digits organized from left to right

half hour - 30 minutes

half past - 30 minutes into an hour

hour - 60 minutes

quarter after - 15 minutes into the hour

quarter to - 15 minutes before the next hour begins

visual schedule - showing pictures of each activity to be completed on a schedule or at least having a schedule in written form

CHAPTER 9

PLAYING WITH YOUR FOOD

We seem to eat more and more meals on the run these days and prepare less and less at home ourselves. The novelty of sitting down to a family dinner loses out to the easy, no fuss on-the-go meal in the car while we rush from point A to point B. Sitting down as a family for meals, whether it be at a restaurant, at home, or with a picnic at the park, is important for fostering communication skills and family interaction, encouraging healthy habits, and developing respect and trust among family members. It allows time to model desired behaviors and slows us down long enough to notice each other. Kids grow up fast. Developing dinner habits now will help bring them back to the table even when they are teenagers with much "more important" things to do. What better way to interact than through food, and how better to do that than by allowing kids to play with their food!

Popular Vocabulary to Sink Your Teeth Into

measurement, weight, ounces, cups, teaspoon, tablespoon, gallon, pint, quart, solid, liquid, gas, greater than, less than, more, size, vary, shades of color, shapes, number, skip counting, clockwise, counterclockwise, density, temperature, even, odd, fractions: half, quarter, eighth, sixteenth

A WORD OF WARNING: KIDS NEED SUPERVISION IN THE KITCHEN WHILE COOKING OR WHILE USING ANY UTENSILS AND SUPPLIES THAT HAVE SHARP EDGES, BLADES, ETC. APPLIANCES MAY BE ENTICING TO KIDS BUT THEY SHOULD

NOT BE USED BY KIDS ALONE. IN ADDITION, MIXING SOME SPICES AND FOODS TOGETHER CAN RESULT IN UNEDIBLE OR STOMACH-TURNING RESULTS. PLEASE USE CAUTION WHEN EXPERIMENTING WITH FOOD WHEN YOU PLAN TO EAT THE RESULT. DO NOT USE INGREDIENTS THAT YOU ARE UNFAMILIAR WITH WITHOUT FINDING OUT MORE INFORMATION ABOUT THEM FIRST. AND OF COURSE, ALWAYS ERR ON THE SIDE OF CAUTION IN THE KITCHEN!!! SAFETY FIRST!!

MEMORABLE MEAL TIME MOMENTS

1. "Weight" for me! Have some fun with food weight and see exactly how much you are eating...and how much you are wasting! Weigh yourself on a bathroom scale before dinner and then again after dinner. What happened? Why? Put all the scraps from each person's plate onto one plate after dinner. Weigh yourself holding an empty plate and then weigh yourself holding the plate of scraps. How much food is going to waste? Have a kitchen scale or some other small scale in the house? Use that to weigh each of your portions. You can weigh the food before it is cooked and again after it is cooked to see what the difference is. Did the weight change, and why? How many ounces are you eating of each item? How much is that altogether?

2. How does your meal measure up? We live in a society where our portions are way too big and our eyes are often bigger than our stomach. Look around the table once everyone is served. Who has the most meat on their plate? Who has the least amount of vegetables? Measure how much you eat by counting how many bites you take of vegetables, meat, carbohydrates, and sugars and chart the results on a bar graph. At the end of the week, see which

foods you ate the most bites of and which foods you ate least. Make a goal for the following week to improve your vegetable intake and make sure you achieve it! You could also lay out your food in lines on plastic wrap and measure the length of each line. Make sure your veggie line is the longest and your sugar line is the shortest. Will you eat your height by the end of the week? Chart it to find out. Ask someone to measure your height, in inches, and then measure your food against your height. How long does it take to eat a line of food as tall as you are? *As a side note, graphs are a difficult concept for many kids to grasp, so the more exposure and experience with them, the better.*

    3.   Search for the colors of the rainbow instead of the pot of gold at the end of it! Eating foods across every food group is important, and so is eating across all colors of the rainbow. Sharpen your color skills with this meal activity. Remember the color wheel and that red, blue, and yellow are primary colors and orange, green, and purple are secondary colors (made by mixing together two primary colors). Keep track of what colors you eat by drawing a rainbow on paper and writing in the foods of that color that you ate during the day. For example, I would write "strawberries" in the red column, "carrots" in orange, "banana" in yellow, "lettuce" in green, "blueberries" in blue, and "eggplant" in purple. See if you can fill the color arch with words by the end of the day for a fulfilled rainbow. Draw a color wheel on another piece of paper and plug in your foods there, too. Talk at meal time about how to eat through more colors the next day. You can also arrange your plate by the order of the color wheel. Place primary colors together, secondary colors under those, and brown/black/white colors in the middle of the plate. (Classify meat based on its color before cooking.) Seem to be eating a lot of

the same colors each night? Go to the grocery store with Mom/Dad next time and help pick some colors of the rainbow that are missing from your plate. Now try separating your plate in half by putting foods that are naturally colored on one side and foods that are artificially colored on the other.

4. Mind your "peas" and "cues". Take a cue from foods on your plate like peas, noodles, rice, corn, and beans. You eat so many of them in a serving that they are begging to be counted. Try skip-counting these foods. Determine what is on your plate that you have an odd number of or an even number of by counting your corn kernels by threes or your noodles by fives. Count beans by twos and peas by fours. You can count on this activity to keep you out of trouble while you eat! All done counting? Count backwards by the same increments as you take each bite. Work sizes in here, too. You can have more corn than anything on your plate, but it may take up the least amount of space on the plate. Try to get an equal number of multiple foods. Can you arrange it so you have 25 spinach leaves and 25 noodles? 14 beans and 14 french fries? Can you work ratios into the dinner plate? Maybe you have eight grains of rice for every bite of meat cut on your plate. What about ounces of milk per teaspoon of applesauce? You can make number and counting connections for just about anything! Mason jars are sturdy glasses that have measurements on the sides making it easy to track your fluid intake. See what possibilities you can come up with. Warning: Kids, if your plate is always consumed with just one item night after night (pizza, hot dog, macaroni), consider talking with the chef about changing up the menu a bit to allow for some more dinner fun! Clip some coupons from the newspaper and make a grocery list from what's on sale at the local grocery market and then offer to go shopping with the cook to help make

some new choices. If you can't do all of these activities during dinner, consider helping with dinner prep and play with everyone's food there! Parents, this is a great way to keep the kids occupied during dinner preparations as well!

5. Fractions pair together with food naturally. What fraction of the pizza did you eat and how many brownies out of the whole did you polish off are easy ones, but how about expanding that? What fraction of the baked potatoes that were made did you consume? What fraction of those potatoes did you consume when they were made into potato fries? What fraction of green beans is still in the serving bowl or the pot when dinner is done? (Yes, that means you need to keep track of how many were dished out...hmmm...seems to me you could do the serving then!) See if you can get a third of your plate to be vegetables and fruit. Try eating in fractions. Eat a fourth of your food and then stop to ask how someone's day was. Separate your pile of mashed potatoes into eighths and after eating each eighth, compliment someone at the table (especially the person who cooked dinner). If you really want to earn a pat on the back, share half of your dessert with someone else at the table!

6. This dinner activity will take a hands-on approach. See how many shapes you can make with your food. Use your hands, fork, knife, cookie cutters, or whatever it takes. Can you make some shapes that no one else thinks of? How about making 3-D shapes? If you are able to help prepare dinner, see how many shapes you can incorporate into the meal. Maybe you can make breadsticks that are polygons. How many shapes can spaghetti noodles make on your plate? Meatballs can be made into cones, cylinders, cubes, and spheres. Can you change the shape of the napkins used tonight when you set the table? How might you add

more shapes to the dinner table with place mats or center pieces?

These six scenarios are just examples and starters to help you understand how you can play with your food and practice some math during meal time with the family. There are thousands of other ways that you can edu-play with your food and make meal time fun. Use the space below to add your own ideas while they are fresh in your mind.

1.

2.

3.

The Smart Home

HOW TO PLAY WITH FOOD…WHEN THE GROWN-UPS ARE WATCHING!

- Make Jell-O® and use cookie cutters or a cheese spreader to make shapes of all kinds.

- Cookie dough can be used to practice learning about area of the cookie, diameter, and radius.

- Any baking can help with measurements and fractions. (teaspoon, tablespoon, cup, half a cup, etc.)

- Setting the table is a great way to introduce symmetry.

- Reading food labels introduces elements of nutrition as well as measuring out serving sizes.

- Serving dessert lends well to talking about "greater than", "less than", or "equal to"; especially among siblings!

- Use different sized dishes at dinner to discuss increases, decreases, reduce/reduction, and size.

- The idea of boiling and evaporation can be introduced when cooking pasta, boiled eggs, or corn on the cob.

- Play with hot and cold and varied temperatures by serving soup and salad for dinner or by mixing hot drinks on a cold night and visa versa.

- Freezing and melting are words and concepts that go well with serving ice in drinks at meal time.

- Relate recipes to formulas when cooking anything.

- Locate a translation guide online or in the front of a cookbook and bake something using grams and kilograms as well as liters to show the differences in measurement systems and translations of them.

- Cleaning up the dishes after meal time lends itself well to ideas of float/sink, waste, friction (scrubbing pots/pans/dishes), absorb, water, depth, and temperature.

- Chemical and physical change can be seen during almost every step of the cooking process for any meal.

- See how energy and movement relate to heat as you bring soups or other liquids to a boil.

- Use old, rarely-used seasonings and expired pantry items for experiments and observations of change instead of just throwing them out.

- Rummage through the refrigerator for sour cream, salad dressings, etc. to show separation, settling, mixtures, physical change, and layers (and clean the fridge while you're at it).

- Break down whole food items in a blender or mixer to show how a whole can take up more or less space than the sum of its parts.

- Cut up vegetables have angles, as do napkins, silverware, some dishes, and crackers or sliced fruit.

- Popcorn is a result of heat or change in temperature.

- Talk about balance with the variety of food groups on each person's dinner plate or go further and balance calories from different foods that are consumed.

- Use all kinds of graphs and charts to keep food diaries, grocery lists, and to keep track of diets. Incorporate talk about x-axis and y-axis, labels, titles, and sequential numeration on these graphs.

- Make your dining room table into a multiplication table using colored tape or post-its.

- Count anything from calories to servings to items to colors that are served at meals.

THE PARENTS' ROLE IN MEAL TIME

Your job while the kids are having fun edu-playing with their food and bugging you in the kitchen is to play with your food, too! You can also engage in explanations and use of vocabulary you want them to learn as well as questioning, wondering and hypothesizing with your child to encourage them to continue exploring. Question what will happen to an ingredient once it is cooked or what effect baking will have on your dinner. Make guesses (hypotheses) prior to the cooking as to how each food will turn out in the end (and I am not talking about a critique of your cooking skills here). Teach kids how to conduct safe food experiments and how to use appropriate tools and measurements when necessary. You will soon find cooking and meal preparation more fun for you, and you will get more help from them!

In addition to engaging in meal time fun, it is your job as the parent to give your child the time to host the trials. Meal time is the perfect time to connect with your family and to interact without interruption (no cell phones or TV during meal time). If you are short on time, consider ordering in or shopping for prepared foods on occasion to cut down on prep time rather than cutting out the valuable time your family has to eat together. If that doesn't work, try doubling up on meal time and homework time. What better way to show how science and math fit in with real life. Talk about hands-on learning and real world experiences! Still struggling to find time for dinner experiments and fun? Decide which days you can set aside more time for different experiments. If Monday is a quiet day, allow more play time while eating on that day. If you work from home on Wednesdays, then maybe that's the day to allow the most time for experimentation. Don't limit yourself to just dinner, though. If breakfast is the meal that you all eat together, use that time for food playing fun. Are there too many cooks in the kitchen? Create a chart that gives each child a day in the kitchen with you and make sure busy days show that kitchen preparation time is all yours. Whose job is it to set the table? Talk with that person while they complete their chore and be keen to all the vocabulary and fun that can be included there.

Are you busy trying to talk out a situation from work or school during dinner? Having company over and you aren't sure how they will feel about everyone having their hands in the food? Discussions about science or math can also happen during clean up time after dinner. Ask your children to show you what they came up with while slurping their spaghetti or pushing around their beets. Remember to give them your full attention while they explain their thoughts and wonders and ask open-ended questions to encourage more discussion. Can't find the time right after dinner? Remember the communication log mentioned in chapter one? That doesn't have to apply just to bath time, you know!

As you know, meal time isn't the only time that this vocabulary can be used. You can incorporate these words and your child's exploration of science, math, reading, and writing into many other parts of your day as well. The more you try different things, the more naturally they will fit into what you do everyday. However you decide to integrate these concepts into your family's lifestyle and routines is up to you. Just remember to keep trying! As a bonus, some of these activities may tempt your children to try new foods as well as getting them to actually EAT at dinner time!

CHAPTER GLOSSARY

bar graph - a graph using parallel bars of different lengths that compare information

chart - a graphic representation of information

clockwise - moving in the direction of the rotation of the hands on a clock

cone - a 3-D shape like an ice cream cone

counterclockwise - moving in the direction that is opposite of the rotation of the hands on a clock

cube - a 3-D shape like dice

cup - 8 ounces

cylinder - a 3-D shape like a can

density - the state of being compact

eighth - one of eight pieces that make up a whole

even - able to be divided by 2 with no remainder

fractions - pieces of a whole

gallon - 4 quarts or 16 cups

gas - a substance that has indefinite expansion

half - one of two pieces that make a up whole

liquid - a fluid that takes the shape of the container that holds it

The Smart Home

measurement - an exact size or amount

odd - the opposite of even; not able to be evenly divided by 2

ounces - a unit of weight equaling 1/16 of a pound-a small amount

pint - 2 cups

polygon - a closed, usually straight figure with three or more sides

primary colors - red, yellow, and blue

quart - two pints or 4 cups

quarter - one of four pieces that make up a whole

secondary colors - colors made when mixing two primary colors (orange, purple, green)

shades of color - varieties of a color (pink, magenta, and ruby are shades of red)

sixteenth - one of sixteen pieces that make up a whole

skip counting - counting by a number that is not one; counting by tens, fives, twos, threes, etc.

solid - a material that holds a definite shape

sphere - a 3-D circle

tablespoon - a measurement of 15 ml (like a large kitchen spoon)

teaspoon - a measurement of 5 ml (like a regular kitchen spoon)

vary - change

Shannon Pretorius

SAFE COOKING

NO BAKE, NO CUT RECIPES FOR KIDS

Cooking is one of the most engaging, fun, experimental activities that I can think of. It brings me together with friends and family, it is soothing when I need something to take my mind off my day, and it lets me be creative and different. Although many don't feel the same way I do about cooking, it is an art that can be wonderful to share with your kids and opens up so many opportunities for communicating and learning together. I thought I would pass along some recipes (if you can call them that) that I enjoy letting my little one make on her own without any blood, sweat, or tears...from either one of us. Her face beams and her confidence soars when she comes to the table with a creation that is all hers and something that we ALL enjoy!

The foods included here are prepared without the need for cutting, and the only heating necessary is done in a microwave. Some of the recipes do call for using a blender. Skip those if you are not comfortable with that. Some of these recipes can be adapted for older kids who may be able to handle using a toaster oven or the stove and could use a butter knife to help cut things. To help bring your munchkins into the kitchen with you, think about foods or meals that your family eats regularly and figure out ways to alter them so the kids can take over preparations, or find jobs within the current preparations that are suitable for your child's age and ability level. The creations in this section are not things I made up. They are regular foods or meals that you may already be preparing.

The Smart Home

Note: Because cooking is all about creativity, I have not included exact measurements in any of these recipes. If an experiment fails, kids will learn about trial and error, changing amounts and adjusting measurements, and paying attention to detail! DON'T FORGET TO INSIST ON HAND-WASHING BEFORE ANY COOKING BEGINS!!! Then step out of the way and let the good times roll.

1. **Smoothies** - These are easy to make in the blender or with a potato masher. Mix some berries (if frozen, microwave them or let them thaw first) with a banana that you mash in your hands. Add some flavored yogurt and a splash of juice or milk. Blend or mash together and enjoy!

2. **Breakfast Parfaits** - Layer granola, toasted oats, or cereal with yogurt and fruit in a cup for an easy parfait.

3. **Fruit Kabobs** - Use toothpicks to spear grapes, mandarin orange slices, and berries to make mini-kabobs. Dip them in fruit yogurt if desired.

4. **Banana Nut Goodies** - Peel a banana and slice it the long way, using a cheese spreader. Spread peanut butter on one cut side of the banana. Sprinkle with nuts, mini chocolate chips, or raisins. Put the other half of the banana back on so you have a banana nut goodie sandwich. What a snack!

5. **Ants on Logs** - Remember good old ants on logs? Wash a stalk of celery, spread peanut butter on it, top with raisins, and crunch! Another variety of that is to put cream cheese on the celery and sprinkle with season salt or a pinch of garlic powder and salt. Or use flavored cream cheese and

forget the seasonings. Yum!

6. **Watermelon Soup** - Puree watermelon chunks in a blender or use a potato masher. Add cream or milk and some Cool Whip if you have some. Add fresh mint or a dash of nutmeg if you wish. Great, easy summer soup!

7. **Layer Dip** - Spread some refried beans on the bottom of a loaf pan or pie plate with a cheese spreader. Peel an avocado and smooth it in a bowl using a fork or your hands. Lay that on top of the beans. Break up some lettuce on top of that, grape tomatoes next, and then drop some spoons of sour cream on top. Sprinkle on some shredded cheese and top with salsa. Enjoy with corn chips.

8. **Veggie Dip** - Mix some sour cream or plain yogurt with whatever seasonings you would like (dried onions or onion powder, garlic powder, salt, pepper, chives, etc.). Dip your favorite raw veggies or pretzels in it.

9. **Roll-ups** - Spread mayonnaise or avocado on a tortilla using a cheese spreader. Pile on cheese, torn lettuce, lunch meat or leftover meat from last night's dinner, and grape tomatoes. Roll it up and share!

10. **Roly-Poly** - Wrap a cheese stick or pickle in some lunch meat or a lettuce leaf. Stick a toothpick through it to hold it.

11. **Chicken Salad** - Put a can of tuna or chicken (or salmon) in a bowl. Season it with salt, pepper, garlic powder, onion powder, parsley, etc. Add a spoonful of mayo, a squirt of lemon juice if you have some, and break apart some celery to add as well. Mix and serve on bread, over crackers, or on

a bed of lettuce.

12. **Snack Mix** - Clear the cupboards of the "almost gone" cereals, nuts, seeds, and candies and make them new again by mixing them all together in a bowl for a home-made snack mix that will be gobbled up.

13. **Popcorn or Cereal Balls** - Pop some microwave popcorn or put some rice cereal in a bowl. Slightly melt a bit of peanut butter in the microwave and add it to the bowl. Mix in a tablespoon of corn syrup if you have some on hand. Fold it all together with a rubber spatula or your hands. Form/press into balls and refrigerate until hardened.

14. **Italian Noodle Salad** - Lay last night's leftover plain noodles (any kind) in a bowl. Break apart some broccoli florets, dump in some grape tomatoes, add some black olives, tear off small pieces of a green onion, and put in whatever other veggies you enjoy. Pour on some Italian dressing and top with shredded parmesan cheese. Mix it up and let it marinate in the fridge for a few hours.

15. **Ramen Salad** - Break apart an uncooked package of Ramen Noodles and place the pieces in a bowl. Add sliced almonds, some sesame oil and sunflower seeds, a little red wine vinegar or some other vinegar of your choice, a bit of sugar, pea pods or bean sprouts or some shredded cabbage, and a little olive oil. Mix it together and refrigerate it for several hours. Eat when you can't stand to wait any longer!

16. **Citrus Salad** - Peel some grapefruit and oranges. Put the segments in a bowl. Add some juice and sprinkle with basil

or mint.

17. **Fresh Tomato Salad** - Helping with dinner couldn't get easier than this one. Wash some grape or cherry tomatoes. Whisk together some balsamic vinegar and olive oil and pour on the tomatoes. Sprinkle with salt. Tear some basil leaves to add to the salad and then sprinkle in some shredded mozzarella cheese. Mix it all together. Presto!

18. **Garbage Nachos** - Put a layer of tortilla chips or broken taco shells on a plate. Top with your choice of leftovers from the refrigerator. Then cover with shredded cheese. Microwave for 30-60 seconds until most of the cheese is just melted. This is a great way to use up leftovers and create a dinner everyone will eat!

19. **Chicken Taco Bowl** - Microwave frozen, precooked grilled chicken strips according to the package directions. Break a taco shell into pieces and place it in a bowl. Top that with torn lettuce, shredded cheese, the chicken strips, and olives (or whatever other taco toppings you desire). Mix and eat.

20. **Vegetable Soup** - Pour some frozen peas, corn, beans, potato chunks, or whatever vegetables you have available into a bowl. Add some chicken or vegetable broth, salt, pepper, onion powder, and parsley. Mix, microwave until warm, and serve.

21. **Pita People** - Separate a piece of pita bread through the pocket so you have two full circles. Spread each with a light layer of cream cheese (which will act as glue). Use shredded cheese to sprinkle on some hair, grape tomatoes or olives for eyes and a nose, and use baby carrots or sweet

pepper strips to form a mouth.

22. **Berry Cheesy Pie** - Soften some cream cheese and thaw some frozen berries (or use fresh, bite-sized berries). Put a layer of graham crackers in the bottom of a pie plate or 8 by 8 pan. Combine the cream cheese with some powdered sugar and a touch of vanilla extract. Mix with a rubber spatula. Spread some of the mixture on top of the graham crackers with the spatula or the back of a spoon. Top with berries and repeat the process for one more layer. Enjoy as a light dessert or a snack!

23. **Ice Cream Cookies** - Scoop some ice cream onto a cookie. Place another cookie on top. Press down lightly. Roll the sides in a treat of your choice such as mini chocolate chips, cake sprinkles, cinnamon candies, etc. Then freeze it until after dinner or just enjoy it now!

24. **Popsicles** - Use an ice cube tray and toothpicks or a plastic container or any other reasonable mold and plastic straws to make this treat. Mix some soft or mashed fruit of your choice with some flavorful juice (and some yogurt if you desire) and pour into the molds. Freeze and eat!

25. **Dessert Dip** - Melt chocolate chips with a small amount of water in the microwave. Dip strawberries, banana pieces, sweet bread, or marshmallows for a delightful dessert!

Food is an amazing avenue that brings people together. All of these recipes can be made with very little or no assistance from an adult. Sit back and enjoy watching your kids come alive in the kitchen with a sense of control, adventure, pride, and satisfaction that will be a recipe for success in their daily lives.

The Smart Home

101 No-Cost Educational Games/Activities for Families to Do Together

Who says nothing in life is free?

1. Make muffins, cakes, or breads with whatever you have in the pantry to practice measurements.

2. Put on a talent show for neighbors and friends to showcase talents of all kinds.

3. Use household items to make instruments and play music in time with a beat.

4. Use short noodles and string to make jewelry or glue the noodles on paper for 3-D art incorporating patterns or shapes (add color to noodles by soaking them in water and food coloring).

5. Play spy games to find shapes and colors.

6. Play music and do directional dancing (clockwise, counterclockwise, to the right, to the left, go north, step south, travel east, wiggle west).

7. Play hopscotch using only odd or even numbers or using words in the boxes.

8. Break into teams and go on a scavenger hunt. Describe

for the other team the objects you found using as many descriptive words as possible without naming the objects. Have the other team guess what they are before showing them.

9. Plan a picnic and assign each person the task of picking one food from a specific food group to create a balanced meal.

10. Take a walk and see how many living and non-living things you can find along the way, tallying them as you go.

11. Use pool play to practice opposites (under, over, low, high...) or distances.

12. Play freeze tag and have the frozen people skip count to 100 to unfreeze.

13. Lay down and watch the clouds on a breezy day, and note how they change shape, color and size as they move across the sky and talk about the directions (north, south, east, west) that they are moving.

14. Read together-you with your book and the kids with theirs. Talk about what you read and your thoughts about it afterwards.

15. Rake the leaves, measure the diameter of the pile in steps, jump in the leaves together and then measure again.

16. Play hide-n-seek with clues of where you will hide. Base the clues on landmarks or paces from certain objects.

17. Play on the swing set, noting heights, distances, speeds,

The Smart Home

and time as you play.

18. Make a map of your house or yard and have your kids find their dessert or a special note by following the map to the destination.

19. Catch bugs in a net or in a jar with a lid and talk about their species, purpose, and body parts before letting them go again.

20. Turn a game of baseball, wiffle ball, basketball, or another kind of ball into a physics lesson.

21. Run through the sprinklers on a sunny day, explaining rainbows and prisms.

22. Make a fort out of blankets in the living room and tell stories to each other inside.

23. Plant a seed from your watermelon, avocado, peach, apple, etc., identifying the process the seed will take to grow.

24. Make simple machines with blocks, empty containers, etc. and put them to use.

25. Make popsicles with ice cube trays, juice, and toothpicks to show changes in states of matter.

26. Fill the sink and drop in objects to see what floats and what sinks. Then make bubbles by adding soap. Wash plastic toys so you don't waste the water.

27. Cut a piece of fruit and put it on a table outside to watch

what insects you attract. Discuss the food chain, insect groups, or life cycles while you watch.

28. Make a telescope out of a paper towel tube or binoculars from toilet paper rolls and tape to watch the bugs that gather during activity 27.

29. Turn on the TV but mute the volume and create your own story about what the characters are saying and doing.

30. Write songs together using rhyming words and make up a tune to go with them. Talk about pitch, volume, amplification, and sound frequency.

31. Make up your own card games to focus on number skills.

32. Host theme days such as beach day or blizzard day and have everything that you do that day and every place you go relate to your theme somehow. Talk about weather, being prepared, and safety throughout the day.

33. Make a family safe box where anyone in the family can write down a thought, concern, idea, etc. Plan one evening a week to eat a favorite meal and discuss what's in the safe box together. Come up with solutions for any issues.

34. Play with your food together at meal time and talk about the ingredients used to make the food and where each ingredient came from.

35. Host relay races where you fill different sized buckets with water using different sized scoops or containers to show what a cup, teaspoon, quart, etc. looks like and when

The Smart Home

we would use each one. Water your plants with the collected water when you are done.

36. Put together a family exercise program that works for everyone and do it 3 times a week.

37. Use shoe boxes to make individual mailboxes and discuss how the mail system works. Then use junk mail envelopes and write letters to each other to fill each person's mailbox.

38. Create a bartering economy within your home to show the basics of economics. You can barter with goods or services.

39. Put a piece of cardboard (toilet paper roll) or thick paper, a penny, a piece of soap, and an aluminum can (or some other empty food container you have) outside on a table or in a tub of sorts to observe and document what happens to each item as the days and weeks go by. Discuss weathering and erosion along with physical and chemical changes.

40. Grocery shop together to work on concepts of money, savings/spending, needs and wants, etc.

41. Have family letter days where you eat foods that start with a certain letter, play games that start with a certain letter, and give compliments that start with a certain letter. This is a great way to increase vocabulary and introduce new foods and activities to the family.

42. Play dice games you have or make up your own to talk

about probability (certain, likely, unlikely...).

43. Watch a subtitled movie together.

44. Make your own Battleship® game to practice grids and ordered pairs by drawing a grid on paper with numbers attached to the lines. Draw a shape or object in 4-5 different places on your grid. Then call out ordered pair coordinates. The other person will make a dot in the spot you named. Decide together how to score points, or just play for fun.

45. Build your own terrarium with an empty plastic bottle, a scoop of soil from outside, and a seed from a flower or piece of fruit you ate.

46. Camp in the backyard and talk about the stars/solar system and weather elements.

47. Make a family calendar together drawing pictures to go with each month. Incorporate seasons and seasonal changes into the pictures and discuss time frames such as year, month, week, and day.

48. Write notes to each other using a code that the other person has to decipher.

49. Collect a sample of rock from different places you go for a week. Study each one to see how the rock was made and how each is the same or different from the next.

50. Make a rock garden or shell garden together with samples you find on your property or with ones you find when you

go places. Leave an area in the middle for cloud watching.

51. Have a family jump rope competition while discussing speed, motion, and stamina as well as practicing coordination.

52. Play on educational websites together and challenge each other to activities on the site.

53. Change the rules to Dominoes® so that you have to match even numbers to odd or you have to use a Domino that has one more or one less dot then the one it's touching.

54. Play charades to practice vocabulary development and communication as well as social interaction.

55. Take old socks and make them into puppets with markers or whatever items you have in your junk drawer that you don't need. Then put on a puppet show. This activity is good for talking about recycling, story telling, story elements, and character development.

56. Reuse the newspaper by making paper hats to wear and paper boats to float in the tub.

57. Go to the park and find simple machines on the playground (see saw, ramp, etc.) while you play and then take a nature walk.

58. Decorate you dinner table by making it into a multiplication table or a map.

59. Watch a family comedy show together (laughing is a very

healthy activity).

60. Build a fire (inside or out) and roast marshmallows or cook dinner on it while discussing heat, melting, boiling, temperatures, and safety rules.

61. Develop a family tree together which will open up talk about generations, relatives, and historical changes in the world over the last hundred years.

62. Look for things that start with every letter of the alphabet as you are driving somewhere.

63. Play the rhyming game in the car. Start with one word and see how many rhymes you can come up with from that word.

64. Build a play dough city together (you can easily make play dough if you don't have any) and talk about grids and planning.

65. Measure things around the house (the TV is six hands long, the couch is three arms long...) and then list them in order from shortest to longest.

66. Make paste and play dough as science projects.

67. Play Monopoly® or Life® or Pay Day®, focusing on economics and the idea of making money to spend money.

68. Play Twister® (easy to make your own if you don't have the game) to work in some healthy stretching and exercise as well as balance.

The Smart Home

69. Paint together. Art is a great educational experience. Try painting one still life and one abstract piece. If you don't have paint or paper, use markers, or use water and paint brushes or sponges on the driveway.

70. Make a family time capsule by having each person pick one thing that is special to him/her. Write a note about each item and put it in a plastic bag before burying everything in the yard. (Watch out for pipes when burying the time capsule.)

71. Encourage second language development by watching the Spanish channel on TV. See how well you can figure out what's going on.

72. Make a train or bus with chairs from around the house and take turns being the engineer, the ticket collector, passenger, etc. to practice turn-taking, routes and maps, directions, and career choices.

73. Play musical chairs.

74. Make a lunar cycle chart by drawing what the moon looks like nightly.

75. Make a map of the United States and try to find license plates from each state while driving through your day. Mark them on the map with a dot or a star when you find them.

76. Challenge each other to see who can withhold from using electricity the longest. Talk about power sources and sources of energy.

77. Use boxes to make a dog house or play house and discuss the angles and measurements needed.

78. Role play using different roles of community helpers so kids understand who to go to for help when they need something.

79. Make collages out of old magazines. Think of a theme for the collage such as alphabet letters, parts of speech (noun, adjective...), activities, etc. or have kids find letters in different fonts to help them recognize different types of print.

80. Doing laundry together is a great way to work on sorting by color or size or material.

81. Bake leftover hard candy on wax paper to make stained glass creations. Show changes in states of matter, reusing and recycling, and light reflection.

82. Play Hangman® to promote phonemic awareness.

83. Make a Venn diagram using yarn, hula hoops, chalk, etc. and use it to compare two items you have at home.

84. Use sticks and acorns or something else from nature to make angles, line segments, shapes, and number lines on the sidewalk.

85. Use an empty can or jar to collect spare change that comes into the house and work on money counting and labeling skills. (OK, so that takes money, but it is your money and it doesn't leave your possession!)

The Smart Home

86. Form cooked spaghetti noodles into different shapes and see how many uses you can come up with for them.

87. Make a chart together naming family chores and responsibilities and review it to make necessary alterations at least monthly.

88. Name 3 random objects (you could write a bunch down and then pick 3 of them out of a hat) and have each person try to come up with something to make from them-this is great for creativity, strategy, and working together.

89. Play Marco Polo without the water by blindfolding someone to have them try to locate you-this works on strengthening your senses.

90. A good ole' game like hot potato works on hand-eye coordination and reflexes as well as sportsmanship and team work.

91. Depending on how many members there are in your family, you can do some team building activities such as trust falls, an obstacle course where everyone has to help everyone else get through it (time yourself), or relay races. These would be great to do with neighbors or other families if you need more participants.

92. Scrabble®, Boggle®, and Alpha Bits® cereal or Scrabble Cheez-Its® are great resources to use to practice spelling, word association, and many other word reading skills.

93. Turn on some music to sing and dance together. Work on

coordination, imitating, stretching, rhythm, and basic dance moves.

94. Start a family court room where one person is the judge, a couple are lawyers, etc. so when sibling squabbles occur, the kids can take it to court and learn about the judicial system first hand.

95. Write your family memoir as it unfolds by journaling together about last week's events. Look at each person's point of view regarding the events that are documented.

96. If you have family pets, there's no better time to teach them tricks and manners then when the family is altogether to participate. Make it into a game show.

97. Have a family yard sale and make some money instead of spending it. Have everyone gather some things together they don't want anymore, make signs to teach advertising, and work on money skills by adding up profits or making change.

98. Use take-out menus to play restaurant at meal time. Planning, math, manners, and mixing ingredients will be taught here.

99. Make family gift lists or wish lists using newspaper ads or commercials seen on TV. Write the name of the item, where to buy it, and the cost.

100. Write a neighborhood chronicle and interview neighbors for articles.

101. Host backwards day to stir up routines. Wear clothes backwards; eat dessert when you wake up and then dinner, moving through the day and finishing off with breakfast before bed.

Add ideas your family comes up with here:

102.

103.

104.

105.

106.

107.

108.

109.

WORDS TO THE WISE...

THAT'S YOU!

Edu-play is the idea of combining education and learning into the natural world of child's play. Thank you for allowing me to introduce this concept to you and for keeping an open mind about how the activities and adventures presented in this book can work for your family. We are all so busy today that the thought of education beyond the school day is enough to make us cringe. A friend of mine, whom I respect greatly, told me that I overlooked a chapter for this book. The chapter would be called "Super Parent". That thought made me picture a parent who is trying to read this book while clearing the dinner dishes, listening to the kids fighting over whose dessert is bigger, tripping over the camping gear that needs to be put away, and staring at a pile of laundry that has grown larger than a 7-year old. Relax. There are times when we cannot handle one more thing...although we still offer to watch the neighbor's kids while they go out for a romantic dinner and help finish the science project that was started the night before it was due. There are other weeks when we have time left at the end of each day, probably because we didn't shower or get dressed that day, the refrigerator is still empty, and the mail has been neglected so long that you can no longer find the desk it is sitting on. Many of us live a life that much resembles a natural disaster, or so it would appear to others. I am not asking you to try to balance one more crystal glass on your towering plate. My challenge to you this month is for you to integrate one element of edu-play from your favorite chapter of this book into what you are already doing. See what happens. Take what you are already doing and make it new

The Smart Home

again. Then next month, try a different activity, or change the way you are using the current idea. Try one new thing each month and let the rest just happen naturally.

Thank you for bringing me into your home and allowing me to suggest changes in the way that you play, for caring enough to experiment with practices that are already running smoothly in your home, and for keeping an open mind. Your kids will learn these skills from you and be better people for it.

I thank you, and your children thank you as well.

www.ingramcontent.com/pod-product-compliance
Lightning Source LLC
Chambersburg PA
CBHW060837050426
42453CB00008B/728